SOME JAPANESE PORTRAITS

SOME JAPANESE PORTRAITS

Donald Keene

Illustrations by Motoichi Izawa

KODANSHA INTERNATIONAL LTD.
Tokyo, New York & San Francisco

Publication of this book was assisted by a grant from the Japan
Foundation.

Distributed in the United States by Kodansha International/USA,
Ltd., through Harper & Row, Publishers, Inc., 10 East 53rd Street,
New York, New York 10022; in Canada by Fitzhenry & Whiteside
Limited, 150 Lesmill Road, Don Mills, Ontario M3B 2T6; in Mexico
and Central America by HARLA S.A. de C.V., Apartado 30–546,
Mexico 4, D.F.; in South America by Harper & Row, International
Department; in the United Kingdom by Phaidon Press Ltd., Littlegate
House, St. Ebbe's Street, Oxford OX1 1SQ; in Continental Europe
by Boxerbooks Inc., Limmatstrasse 111, 8031 Zurich; in Australia
and New Zealand by Book Wise (Australia) Pty. Ltd., 104–8 Sussex
Street, Sydney 2000; in the Far East by Toppan Company (S) Pte.
Ltd., No. 38, Liu Fang Road, Jurong, Singapore 22.

Published by Kodansha International Ltd., 2–12–21 Otowa, Bunkyo-
ku, Tokyo 112 and Kodansha International/USA, Ltd., 10 East 53rd
Street, New York, New York 10022 and 44 Montgomery Street, San
Francisco, California 94104. Copyright in Japan 1978 by Kodansha
International Ltd. All rights reserved. Printed in Japan.

LCC 76–39679
ISBN 0–87011–298–8
JBC 1095–785725–2361

First edition, 1978

To
Ariyoshi Sawako
for kind words
when I needed them

CONTENTS

PREFACE

Several years ago, when I was asked by the editor of the Japanese weekly magazine *Shūkan Asahi* for a series of "promenades" through Japanese literature, I decided to write about authors, rather than about representative works. This approach, though not unknown in Japan, especially when dealing with twentieth-century literature, is relatively unusual, and I thought it might intrigue readers. My choice of figures also seems to have surprised many people. Some of my "portraits" were of writers well-known even to persons of relatively modest literary background, but others were of figures (like Shōtetsu or Ōnuma Yūko) who hardly exist even as names to the average reader. I confess that it gave me peculiar pleasure to think of introducing to the mass audience of a weekly magazine writers so remote from the selection of film stars, baseball players, and successful businessmen more commonly featured in its pages.

Of course, it was not solely the desire to astonish readers that governed my choice of figures. A few, like the first (Ikkyū) and the last (Masaoka Shiki), were chosen because I had long been interested in these men. But in general, my intent was to present a variety of authors for each of the periods treated in order to suggest the richness and diversity of Japanese literature during that age. In the selection of fifteenth-century writers, for example, there is one poet who wrote in Chinese, another who wrote *waka* (the classic Japanese verse form), and a third who was a poet of *renga* (linked verse), as well as a dramatic poet. If there had been a fifteenth-century fiction writer of distinction, I would certainly have been glad to include him, but I do not know of any. In the following periods the selections were expanded from four to five or six in order to cover more adequately the greater variety of literature that was composed.

The order of the portraits is not always chronological. After writing about Ikkyū it was natural to write next about Sōchō, a poet whose life was colored by his great admiration of Ikkyū, though he was considerably younger than the next two men I sketched. Departures from chronological order in later sections have been governed by similar considerations. I tried rearranging the portraits in strict chronological order when preparing this edition, but I became aware then of underlying themes that linked one portrait to the next. Without changing my conception of the book it would not be easy to change the order of the figures presented.

Another problem has been how to designate the periods to which the different clusters of figures have been assigned. When I published the first group of four portraits in Japanese they were labeled as Muromachi period writers, and the second group appeared as Sengoku period figures. But I became aware this time that three of my four Muromachi men wrote much of their best work after 1467, the year of the outbreak of the Ōnin War, which is often taken to mark the end of the Muromachi period. The inability of historians to agree on a terminal date for the Muromachi period and the beginning of the Sengoku period similarly makes my Sengoku figures rather uncertain representatives of their age. I have found it more convenient, therefore, to use the Western chronological divisions of fifteenth and sixteenth centuries in place of Muromachi and Sengoku periods. For the two later sections I was able to follow traditional Japanese nomenclature without great difficulty, and I have used the term Kinsei for the literature composed between 1600 and 1867, and the term Meiji for literature composed between 1868 and 1912. However, even in the latter case I have been somewhat unconventional in that I have chosen to conclude my essays about 1900, rather than continue to the end of the Meiji period. These portraits, then, extend over the five hundred years from 1400 to 1900. I realize that some readers may be disappointed not to have the entire range of Japanese literature represented, but half a millenium is surely more than enough for one author to attempt to cover!

My intent, as it will soon be obvious, has not been to present a series of biographies in the manner of encyclopaedia articles. This kind of biography writing is of course valuable, but my attention has been drawn to the particular twenty-one writers I have treated because of larger issues that seem to arise from their lives and works. For example, during the sixteenth century, a period of almost unbroken warfare, writers were constantly faced with the problem of how to survive while maintaining some measure of dignity. In the Kinsei period the problems were more varied; those I have treated include: what it meant to be the disciple of a great poet; the importance of rivalry as necessary stimulus to excellence; the continuing validity of the *waka*, a poetic form which had been perfected a thousand years earlier; and the reasons why Japanese of the period wrote much poetry in Chinese, a foreign language that none of them spoke. I have been more attracted to such issues than to details of the biographies of the writers I have chosen to portray.

It will be noted that I have not treated many extremely famous Japanese writers of the five hundred years I have covered. However, even though I made no separate portraits for Saikaku, Bashō, or Chikamatsu, writers I have discussed at length elsewhere, I feel sure that their presence will be detected in my accounts of their rivals and disciples.

For the benefit of those readers not familiar with the literary background of the four periods dealt with, I have prefaced each group of portraits with a brief account.

DONALD KEENE
Tokyo–New York–Tokyo

THE FIFTEENTH CENTURY

At the beginning of the fifteenth century Japan was stronger
and enjoyed a more thriving culture than in many years. Not long
before, in 1392, the country had been reunited after almost sixty
years of division between two rival imperial courts, the Northern
and Southern. The reunification was effected by the shogun,
Ashikaga Yoshimitsu (1358–1408), who was not only one of the
most powerful men of Japanese history but an outstanding connoisseur of the arts. Yoshimitsu resigned as shogun in 1394, but
continued to exert power behind the scenes. The Chinese, to
whom Yoshimitsu sent embassies early in the fifteenth century,
referred to him as "King of Japan," and he did not reject the
appellation.

Sporadic fighting went on in various parts of the country, but
on the whole peace prevailed. This happy situation did not last
long. Yoshimitsu's successors included some able men, but most
of the fifteenth-century shoguns were cruel and capricious and
lacked either the intelligence or the purpose to maintain a strong
regime.

In 1467, the first year of the Ōnin period, the Ōnin War broke
out between the supporters of the two rival heirs to Ashikaga
Yoshimasa, the shogun at the time. The warfare was mainly
waged in the streets of Kyoto, the capital. Almost every building
in the city was destroyed in the course of the fighting, which lasted
until 1477, when the rival armies marched away, having decided
nothing. Many treasures of art and literature perished in the
flames, and the city did not fully recover for over a century. The
writers of the capital were driven by the warfare to different parts
of the country, where they sought the protection of local rulers.
In return they brought to the provinces much of the traditional
culture that had been confined to people associated with the court.

The most typical literary art of the century was *renga*, or linked verse. Several men took turns at supplying "links" in fourteen or twenty-one syllables to the previous verse, the content and even the wording of each successive link being governed by elaborate rules of composition. No doubt the pleasure of companionship accounted for much of the popularity of *renga* in an age of warfare and mutual distrust. But the destruction of culture should not be overemphasized: the Nō drama flourished, and the Buddhist monasteries were bastions of culture, especially with respect to the reading and writing of Chinese.

The century ended with fresh disasters, notably the famine of 1499 which brought death to many. When the Emperor Go-Tsuchimikado died in 1500 his body could not be buried for months because there was not enough money to pay for the funeral expenses. Seldom has a century so promisingly begun ended so badly.

IKKYŪ

1394–1481

Some years ago, after a talk I gave to New York City high school teachers on the characteristics of Japanese literature, one teacher asked, "What has Japanese literature in the way of biography?" I was unable to supply an immediate answer because I had never even considered the question. I could not recall ever having seen a special section in a history of Japanese literature devoted to biography, though of course there are many accounts of great men of the past. The first example that came into my head that day was the description of the death of the despot Taira no Kiyomori in *The Tale of the Heike*. As a story it is superb, but it cannot be accepted as biography in the strict sense. Nor can the legends about the martial hero Yoshitsune, though they have fascinated Japanese readers for centuries and have provided storytellers and playwrights with a seemingly inexhaustible source of materials, be considered as biography, at least as this term is used of Plutarch's *Parallel Lives of the Greeks and Romans,* admired and imitated for almost two thousand years in the West. The New Testament is a kind of biography, as are the accounts that form a whole library of lives of the saints. Ever since the Renaissance, which brought about a rediscovery of the individual, biography has occupied an especially prominent position in Western literature. Today when annual literary prizes are awarded in the West, there is almost always one especially for biography.

In Japan biographies of a sort have been written about famous men ever since the seventh-century regent Shōtoku Taishi. These have generally been brief accounts that open with a list of all the names by which a man was known, continue with evidence of his childhood precocity, then present a rapid summary of highlights of the man's career. Like the portraits painted of the same men, the biographies are "official" and give no indication of personal traits such as a bad temper, cowardice, or even humor. We are told only what is necessary in order to convince us that a particular man embodied certain conspicuous virtues or vices. Minamoto Yoritomo, both in his biography and his portraits, emerges as a general and statesman of impressive willpower, but little information is given to us about his personal life.

There does exist in Japan, however, a kind of writing that can be considered as autobiographical—the diaries of the court ladies of the tenth and eleventh centuries. Unlike the official biographies that describe the external events affecting a man's life but not his innermost thoughts, these diaries rarely exhibit any interest in the external world, but are almost entirely personal. The subjectivity of these diaries undoubtedly accounted for the development in eleventh-century Japan of such works of psychological fiction as *The Tale of Genji* or *Nezame Monogatari* (The Tale of Nezame), which are not narrations of adventures, in the manner preferred by storytellers all over the world, but are accounts of believable people leading relatively uneventful lives, seen from the inside.

These diaries differ from true diaries in that they were normally not written down from day to day but long after the events described had occurred. Inevitably, fictional elements crept into the account, whether because of lapses in memory or because the writer's sense of artistic effectiveness induced her to depart from the facts. The author of The Gossamer Years, known as the "Mother of Michitsuna," declared at the outset of her work that her dissatisfaction with the fabrications of the romancers had led her to give this account of what the life of a gentlewoman is really like; but she had to admit that even this work was not free from touches of fiction. Despite the presence of novelistic elements—surely, however, no more numerous than in Cellini's Autobiography or Rousseau's Confessions—we are left with an unforgettable portrait of the "Mother of Michitsuna." Other court ladies continued the tradition of the diary-autobiography until the beginning of the fourteenth century, when The Confessions of Lady Nijō, a stunning example of the genre, was composed.

Even though these works provide us with haunting evocations of the lives of the court ladies who wrote them, they tended to develop into introspective fiction rather than into true biographies. We know even less about the lives of most of the great figures of Japanese history. Perhaps the first person for whom it is possible to write a genuine biography is the celebrated poet Matsuo Bashō (1644–94). There are gaps in our knowledge of his life, but we know incomparably more about him, both externally and internally, than about any of his contemporaries, let alone the prominent statesmen of the remote past, thanks to his letters and diaries and to the reminiscences of the poet left by his disciples. Yet only in recent years have scholars attempted to write a systematic biography of Bashō.

Why did the art of biography develop so slowly in Japan? Perhaps it is because a biography must describe its subject as an individual, and individuality was not a quality emphasized by the Japanese of feudal times. Even in portraiture it is almost impossible to distinguish among the faces of, say, the thirty-six "immortals of poetry," depicted in many works of art. About the most an amateur can do is to tell the men and women apart, but not even this is easy in some cases: in the *ukiyoe* by such masters as Harunobu and Utamaro the young men and women are often depicted with almost identical features, as if the artist's conception of beauty was more important to his pictures than any suggestion of individuality.

Something resembling individuality did, however, exist in Japan, the tradition of eccentricity. In a feudal society where conformity was demanded of its members, people tended to behave in a manner appropriate to their age, occupation, and status in society without much display of strong individuality; the puppet theater of the eighteenth century with its limited variety of personalities, each clearly expressed by features of the puppet head, was perhaps the most congenial dramatic art for expressing the temper of the times. But the eighteenth century was also a golden age for eccentrics, and their antics were indulgently observed and reported by chroniclers. These eccentrics were certainly not typical of their society, but their unconventionality is appealing, and their quirks of behavior make us feel that we are in the presence of human beings in all their contradictions and unpredictability.

Not all the figures treated in the pages of this book were eccentrics. Indeed, most of them probably thought of themselves as pillars of orthodoxy, though we may not agree with their evaluation. It is fitting, however, to begin with a truly great eccentric, the priest Ikkyū. It would not be possible to write biographies of many priests of his time, but it is possible to write one of Ikkyū, not only because the events of his life and his opinions, as reflected in his poetry and other writings, are interesting in themselves, but because a great many legends and anecdotes have arisen about him. When I read his poetry I seem to hear a living person directly addressing me, and his portraits, filled with life and individuality, produce a similar impression.

Ikkyū was born on New Year's Day in 1394. His father was the Emperor Go-Komatsu, his mother a member of a distinguished branch of the Fujiwara family which had served the rival Southern Court before the country was unified in 1392. Ikkyū's rather plebeian features, as depicted in many portraits, do not suggest exalted lineage, and some historians have discounted the old accounts of Ikkyū's birth. But there is evidence in Ikkyū's poetry that he believed himself to be of imperial stock, and he often visited the palace to see the emperor. When Go-Komatsu was dying in 1433, Ikkyū was summoned to his bedside. Ikkyū, however, was not reared as an imperial prince. Before he was born, his mother had to leave the palace, reputedly because the empress had denounced her as still harboring Southern Court sympathies. We know little else about Ikkyū's mother apart from the letter she wrote him shortly before her death. In this remarkable document she urged him to become so outstanding a priest that he might look down on Shakyamuni Buddha and the Buddhist saint Bodhidharma as his servants.

At the age of five Ikkyū was sent by his mother to a temple as a page, with the expectation he would prepare to become a priest. He showed unusual aptitude in his studies. At the age of eleven he attended lectures on the *Vimalakirti Sutra*, one of the most important texts of Mahayana Buddhism, and in the following year he began his study of the art of composing Chinese poetry, an accomplishment expected of learned priests. Ikkyū's exceptional piety and strict observance of the monastic rules while a student was in contrast with his later reputation as a profligate who paid no attention to normally observed discipline. He spent four years studying under Ken'ō, a monk known for his especially pure character. Ikkyū was desolate when his master died in 1414, and he spent a week in meditation by the shores of Lake Biwa before finally deciding to commit suicide by throwing himself into the lake. He was saved by a man sent by his mother who, knowing of his despondency, had feared he might turn to self-destruction.

Ikkyū, having given up thoughts of suicide, decided in the next year to study under Kasō Sōdon (1351–1428), a Zen master known for his severe discipline. For a long time Kasō refused to admit Ikkyū into his presence, but the young man persisted. One day, on leaving the temple, Kasō noticed Ikkyū was waiting by the gate, and he ordered an attendant to throw water on him. Ikkyū was still waiting when Kasō returned. This time Kasō admitted him to the temple and accepted him as his pupil.

In 1418, when Ikkyū was twenty-four, Kasō bestowed on him the name by which he has since been known. The meaning of the name Ikkyū ("a pause") is suggested by the following poem composed by Ikkyū:

uroji yori	From the world of passions
muroji e kaeru	I return to the world be-
hito yasumi	yond passions,
ame furaba fure	A moment of pause.
kaze fukaba fuke	If the rain is to fall, let it fall;
	If the wind is to blow, let it blow.

The poem is based on the Zen concept that the material and non-material worlds are both essential. One must constantly pass from one world to the other, but in between them, in the pause that refreshes, is pure freedom, and an indifference to rain, wind, or any other external force.

Two years later, in 1420, Ikkyū experienced enlightenment. Late one summer night, when rain clouds hung low over Lake Biwa, he was sitting in Zen meditation in a small boat when he heard the cawing of a crow, and he cried out in wonder. He felt that all his uncertainties had been purged away. When he told Kasō what had happened, the latter said merely, "You have attained the status of an arhat. You are still not a man of supreme accomplishment." Ikkyū replied, "If that is the case, I am delighted to be an arhat and have no desire to be a man of supreme accomplishment." Kasō responded, "You are truly a man of supreme accomplishment."

In 1422, during a ceremony held at the Daitoku-ji, Ikkyū appeared in a shabby, discolored priest's robe and battered straw sandals. All the other priests were dressed in magnificent brocades in honor of the occasion. When Kasō asked why he had chosen such an undignified costume, Ikkyu replied, "I alone ornament this assembly. I have no intention of aping the ways of false priests." After the ceremony somebody asked Kasō if he had decided on a successor. He answered, "Ikkyū, though he acts like a madman."

Ikkyū's "madness" was the expression of unending rage over the stupidity and corruption of the priesthood. He took for his sobriquet the name Kyōun, "crazy cloud," and the character kyō, "crazy," is sprinkled throughout his poetry. In his revolt against the hypocrisy of other priests, who pretended to lead the lives of saints, he went to the opposite extreme. After leaving Kasō's temple, a few years before Kasō's death, Ikkyū openly gave himself to sensual pleasures. In 1440, when services for the thirteenth anniversary of the death of Kasō were held at the Daitoku-ji, parishioners from Sakai assembled at the temple with lavish gifts for the priests. Ikkyū, who had intended to become the superior of the branch temple where the services were held, was so irritated by the unseemly behavior of both parishioners and priests that he left the temple after ten days of noisy celebrations. Before leaving he pasted two poems on the wall. The more sarcastic was addressed to Yōsō, also a disciple of Kasō:

> After ten days of living in this temple my mind's in turmoil;
> Red strings, very long, tug at my feet.
> If one day you get around to looking for me,
> Try the restaurants, the drinking places, or the brothels.

The "red strings" of the second line refer to the ties of physical attachment to women that drew Ikkyū from the temple to the pleasure quarters. The last line was not merely an expression of his contempt for the rules that prohibited priests from eating fish, drinking saké, and indulging in sexual intercourse; Ikkyū's collection of poems in Chinese, *Kyōun Shū* (Crazy Cloud Collection), is filled with extraordinarily frank declarations of delight in pleasures of the flesh:

The Brothel
To lie with a beautiful woman—what a deep river of love!
Upstairs in the brothel a whore and an old Zen priest are
singing.
I derive such pleasure from her embraces and kisses
I've never once thought of renouncing the flames of passion.

Undoubtedly these avowals of indiscretions were intended partly to mock other priests, who secretly indulged in the same pleasures. Of all the priests Ikkyū subjected to his merciless criticism, none fared worse than Yōsō (1376–1458), the twenty-sixth abbot of the Daitoku-ji, whom Ikkyū reviled as a poisonous snake, a seducer, and a leper. In order to rebuild the Daitoku-ji after a disastrous fire that leveled the temple, Yōsō enlisted the support of well-to-do laymen, and was so successful in his endeavor that the court bestowed on him a title never before given to a living abbot of the Daitoku-ji. Ikkyū, however, was sure that Yōsō was extorting money from merchants by promising to secure their enlightenment in return, and he felt revulsion at what he considered to be attempts on Yōsō's part to prostitute Zen for material gains. Yōsō died at the advanced age of eighty-two under circumstances not explained by his official biography, but in *Jikai Shū* (Collection of Self-Admonitions), written in 1455, three years before Yōsō's death,[1] Ikkyū gave a most graphic description of Yōsō's horrible suffering before he died of leprosy. Over a hundred poems in this collection reiterate Ikkyū's conviction that Yōsō was an unparalleled villain. Ikkyū subsequently directed his venom at Yōsō's disciple Shumpo (1410–96), the fortieth abbot of the Daitoku-ji, whose fund-raising activities seemed no less odious than Yōsō's. Ikkyū's attacks so enraged Shumpo's followers that in 1457 an attempt was made on his life.

Ikkyū's attacks on Yōsō were intemperate and probably unfair, but they reveal his uncompromising insistence on maintaining the spirit of Zen. His harsh criticisms extended even to his own life and writings:

Self-Admonition
Master Ikkyū's sins and errors fill the universe
Though the world recognizes him as the master of his sect.
He explains Zen, scolds people, is a master of prosody,
But he may also serve in perpetuity as a master of hell.

At seventy-six Ikkyū fell in love with a blind woman named Mori[2] and wrote about her some of his most affecting poems, including:

After the tree withered and the leaves had fallen, spring returned;
The old trunk has flowered, old promises are renewed.
Mori—if ever I should forget how much I owe you,
May I be a brute beast through all eternity!

Despite his love for Mori and other women (and also boys), Ikkyū remained convinced that human beings were no more than skeletons clothed in flesh. His curious work *Gaikotsu* (Skeletons), written in 1457, described under the guise of a dream about skeletons his belief that the beauty and glory of this world are illusions. "What man can help but be a skeleton? Men and women fall in love because the bones are hidden beneath the outer skin, but when the breath stops and the body disintegrates, such externals disappear. You cannot tell then who once was mighty and who was base. Remember that under the skin you fondle lie the bones, waiting to show themselves."

Skeletons is illustrated with drawings reminiscent of European

depictions of the Dance of Death. In one, skeletons–pallbearers–
carry a third skeleton over whom an elaborate priestly robe has
been thrown. A poem near the drawing asks, "Why should you
decorate the temporary outer form? Don't you know in advance
it will come to this?" For Ikkyū, seeing meaningless pretense
everywhere, the external trappings of religion were but skin
covering the bones. A famous anecdote tells how Ikkyū once appeared in his usual shabby costume to offer a service for a rich
man. The man, annoyed at Ikkyū's lack of dignity, sent him away.
Ikkyū reappeared, this time in splendid attire, and was welcomed
in. He thereupon removed his outer robe and offered it homage.

Ikkyū's *Skeletons* must have seemed a terrifyingly prophetic
book to people of the following decades. In 1460 typhoons and
floods kept crops from ripening and led to a famine in which many
people perished. During the next year an outbreak of epidemics
brought even greater suffering. People turned in desperation
to cannibalism, and skeletons in the tens of thousands lay in the
streets of the capital. In 1464 a religious war broke out between
monks of the Tendai and Shin sects, and there was violence among
the lower classes in the capital. In 1467 the Ōnin War, which destroyed virtually every building in Kyoto, erupted, and most of
the population fled the city. The list of disasters could be prolonged
to fill almost every year left in Ikkyū's long life. Read in this
light, Ikkyū's poems about Mori acquire special poignance.

It is a pity that no proper biography of Ikkyū was written while
the facts were all known, but even from what we can reconstruct
from the poems alone he emerges as a man of particular intensity
who speaks to us across the centuries in a language we can understand with a voice uniquely his own.

NOTES

1. Although *Jikai Shū* as a whole seems to have been written in 1455, Ikkyū may have inserted the section about Yōsō's death later. His mention of the exact date of Yōsō's death certainly was later than the poems attacking him.

2. The name is read Shin by most scholars, but Mori seems to me a more likely pronunciation.

Ikkyū's tomb at Shūon-an

The garden of Shūon-an

SŌCHŌ

1448–1502

Renga (linked verse) is now a virtually extinct literary art. Almost no one today knows its complicated rules, and although a small number of people still amuse themselves by composing poetry which on the surface resembles renga, there are no professional masters, and nobody today seeks to express his deepest emotions in this form. In the Muromachi period, however, renga was the main form of poetic art. The Shogun Yoshimasa composed renga even as the city of Kyoto was burning down around him during the Ōnin War in a Japanese equivalent of Nero playing the fiddle as Rome burnt. Members of the nobility, from such exalted men as the chancellor Nijō Yoshimoto (1320–1398) down, eagerly vied with one another to attract the leading renga poets to their mansions. Even in an age when birth counted for a great deal, it was possible for a man like Sōgi, who came from an extremely obscure family, to be lionized as the arbiter of poetic taste only because of his skill at composing *renga*.

It was not only the nobles and the military leaders who enjoyed composing *renga*. Even in the remote countryside *renga* was a craze. Descriptions of *renga* gatherings, whether held at the court or in some village, suggest that they were often extremely lively. It became customary to award prizes for the best verses, and people placed bets on the verses most likely to win. *Renga* gatherings often turned into gambling parties, and they were accompanied by wine, women, and song. The association of *renga* and gambling was so strong that in the sixteenth century it became necessary at times to prohibit *renga* because of the undesirable riffraff that the gatherings attracted.

It is not surprising that in an age of constant warfare men sought the solace of joining with other men in the peaceful and pleasurable task of composing poetry together. For such men it did not matter too much whether or not the poetry was of high quality. For the average participant in a *renga* session the main consideration was having fun with friends. They were quite satisfied if the *renga* they composed obeyed the rules in general. The first man composed the *hokku* (opening verse) in seventeen syllables, the next man the *wakiku* (second verse) in fourteen syllables, the next man the third verse in seventeen syllables, and so on. There had to be some link between each verse and the one before it. Sometimes this connection (*yoriai*) was merely verbal in the form of a play on words; sometimes it depended on the continuation of the meaning of the previous verse; and in the most exalted cases the link was provided by the "perfume" or overtones of the previous verse. The links tended to be humorous and sometimes indecent. Immense numbers of *renga* sequences of this kind were composed, but almost none have been preserved, no doubt because the poets did not consider them to possess sufficient literary value to warrant their being recorded.

In contrast to this frivolous *renga* there was an elegant and re-

fined variety composed in strict compliance with the codes of composition (*shikimoku*) that had evolved over the years. By the middle
of the Muromachi period there were so many rules that not even
professional poets could hope to know them all. The evolution
of such codes of composition may have originally been intended
mainly to make the game more challenging to experts, but they
resulted in raising the literary level of *renga* by restricting partic-
ipation to poets capable of complying with the complex rules.
The mainstream of *renga* composition thus came to be directed
towards creating a poetic form marked by the beauty and serious-
ness that had characterized the Japanese court poetry of the past.

The greatest of the serious *renga* poets was Sōgi (1421–1502).
He lived in especially turbulent times, and was forced to flee the
capital during the Ōnin War. He became known as a traveler–poet
and left accounts of his journeys to many parts of Japan. But we
know few facts about Sōgi before he was forty. There is little
biographical information even for his later years, and the most we
can infer of a personal nature is that he must have enjoyed robust
health to have traveled so much. Sōgi's poetry is extremely beautiful, and he displayed greater skill at the composition of long
sequences of *renga* than any other poet, but it is hard to detect any
individuality. His teacher Shinkei (1406–75) once wrote, "The
supreme *renga* is like a drink of plain boiled water. It has no
particular flavor, but one never wearies of it, no matter when one
tastes it." This was exactly true of Sōgi's *renga*, and his biography
too is that of a skillful poet rather than that of an interesting man.

Sōgi's disciple Sōchō, however, emerged both in his poetry and
his prose as a distinctive personality. His place in Japanese literary
history has been relatively obscure because he was overshadowed
by Sōgi, but he deserves greater recognition not only because he
was an unusually interesting man but because it is possible to trace
a direct line of descent from Sōchō's *renga* in the comic style to the
haikai poetry that would be perfected by Bashō one hundred and
fifty years later.

In his journal *Utsuyama no Ki* (Utsuyama Account), written in 1517, Sōchō gave a brief autobiographical account of himself. He related that he was born the son of an unskilled artisan. This was apparently his modest way of referring to the fact that he was born into a hereditary family of swordsmiths. His family lived in the province of Suruga, near the present city of Shizuoka, and Sōchō felt a deep attachment to his birthplace. At eighteen he became a priest. Soon afterwards, in 1467, the Ōnin War began, and there was fighting in his province. Sōchō himself took part in the warfare. We do not know exactly what his duties were when he "mingled with the dust of the encampments," but on occasion he composed *renga* sequences to pray for victory or to thank the gods for success in battle. He was close to the Daimyo Imagawa Yoshitada (1442–76), as we know from a statement in *Sōchō Shuki* (Sōchō's Notebook) which mentions that he served at Yoshitada's side day and night for many years. This diary reveals an unusual interest in military information such as the strength of fortifications or the depth of moats, suggesting that Sōchō may have profited by the relative freedom with which *renga* masters could travel around the country to serve as a spy for his master.

When Yoshitada was killed in battle in 1476, a dispute broke out over who should succeed him, his infant son Imagawa Ujichika or his brother. Sōchō, apparently reluctant to become involved in the dispute, went to Kyoto. Another reason for going there was to study under Sōgi. Their first meeting seems to have occurred in 1466. When Sōgi was passing through Okitsu on his way to the east, Sōchō invited him to a *renga* party at the famous temple Seiken-ji. They met again ten years later. Sōgi was then at the height of his fame, both as a poet and as an expert in the Japanese classics. The two quickly became intimate friends. In 1478, when Sōgi journeyed to Echigo, he took Sōchō along, and in 1480 they traveled together to Yamaguchi and northern Kyushu.

Sōchō spent much of the next thirty years in travel. He returned occasionally to Suruga and received financial support from Imagawa Ujichika, who had become the daimyo after the dispute was settled, but his main source of income was probably the gifts he received from the daimyos with whom he composed *renga*. Gradually he established a reputation for himself in the capital, and in 1448 he, Sōgi, and Shōhaku (1443–1527) collaborated in composing *Minase Sangin* (Three Poets at Minase), the most celebrated of all *renga* sequences. At this time he was perhaps slightly inferior to the other two poets, but they were almost equals; if not, the sequence could never have achieved its reputation. By the time of the next collaboration of the three men, when they composed *Yunoyama Sangin* (Three Poets at Yunoyama) in 1491, Sōchō was on equal terms with the others.

Sōchō's close relationship with Sōgi lasted until the latter's death in 1502. Sōchō accompanied Sōgi on his final journey, and was at his side when Sōgi died near Hakone. His account of Sōgi's death, *Sōgi Shūen Ki* (An Account of Sōgi's Death; 1502), is a moving tribute to the master. After Sōgi's death Sōchō was unquestionably the best *renga* poet, but he refused the honors that came his way, preferring to withdraw to a hermitage in his native province. In the following year, as he related in his autobiography, he became acquainted with a woman who washed and sewed his clothes, and eventually two children were born. Of course such relations were prohibited for a Buddhist priest, but Sōchō had never led a monastic life and his formal religious ties were minimal. Perhaps the example of the wayward Ikkyū also inspired him.

When Sōchō first went to Kyoto in 1476, he had headed directly for the Daitoku-ji in order to find Ikkyū. Ikkyū was already eighty-two years old and had only five more years to live. During this period Sōchō was often away from the capital, traveling with Sōgi, so the time the two men could have spent together was limited. Yet Ikkyū's influence on Sōchō dominated him for the rest of his life.

An extreme example of Sōchō's devotion to the memory of Ikkyū is found in an entry in his journal for 1526. A messenger arrived at the Shūon-an, the temple between Kyoto and Osaka which Ikkyū rebuilt in 1456, where Sōchō was staying, with word that Imagawa Ujichika had suddenly died. It was Sōchō's urgent duty to return to Suruga, as his close relationship to the daimyo commanded, but he decided not to go. He had made up his mind that he would die either at the Daitoku-ji or else, like Ikkyū himself, at the Shūon-an. When he left Suruga earlier that year for the capital it was in the belief that he had little time left to live, and he could not risk the possibility of dying elsewhere.

Sōchō's devotion to Ikkyū revealed itself in many ways. He repeatedly contributed money for the rebuilding of temples associated with Ikkyū. In 1525 he sold his prize possession, a set of *The Tale of Genji*, to raise money for this purpose. He also commissioned an artist to paint a portrait of Ikkyū with a long sword in a vermillion scabbard. This portrait was hung in the Shūon-an. Sōchō mentions worshipping the portrait and offering incense before it in 1526 when he returned from a long journey from Suruga. He was exhausted, but when he saw Ikkyū's portrait he felt that weight of old age fall from his shoulders. Some years later he composed this *waka* about the portrait:

uchiharau	The great sword in its
yuka no atari ni	scabbard
oku tachi no	Resting on the clean-swept
sayaka ni izuko	floor
kumoru chiri naki	Is brilliantly clear;
	Nowhere is it clouded
	By a particle of dust.

Mention of the sword obviously stands for Ikkyū's mind, brilliantly clear and sharp.

Sōchō also shared Ikkyū's fondness for playing the *shakuhachi*, for the tea ceremony, and for Nō. These preferences undoubtedly stemmed from Sōchō's own temperament, but the knowledge that Ikkyū shared his tastes probably reinforced them. But it was especially his defiance of convention, so unusual in a poet who was a disciple of Sōgi, that reflected the influence of Ikkyū, who delighted in shocking his fellow priests. Sōchō's admission that he had had two children by a washerwoman is in the vein of Ikkyū, and there is an overtly sexual, sometimes salacious, side to his poetry. In his journal *Sōchō Nikki* (Sōchō's Diary), written when in his eighties, Sōchō confessed that he had turned increasingly to "wild writings," giving this example:

negawaku wa	I only hope and pray
naki na tataji	I won't get a false reputa-
ware shinaba	tion:
yaso amari wo	If I should die
kami mo shiraji yo	I'm sure the gods won't realize
	I was over eighty years old!

The poem suggests that his conduct, even at that advanced age, was such that rumors were likely to spread. A more earthy poem was written after he fell from his horse in 1524 and was unable to use his right hand:

ika ni sen	What am I to do?
mono kakisusabu	Without the hand I use to write
te wa okite	write
hashi toru koto to	For my amusement,
shiri noguu koto	How can I hold my chopsticks
	Or wipe my behind?

The journal often mentions the pleasure Sōchō took in composing *renga* of the *mushin* (or *haikai*) style. He spent the last days of 1523 at the Shūon-an where he and some cronies composed such examples as:

chigo ka onna ka	Is it a boy or a girl
nete no akatsuki	Sleeping there? The morn-
mae ushiro	ing after.
saguru te ni tsuki no	On my hand that gropes
ariake ni	Before and behind, the light
	Of the moon at dawn.
hito no nasake ya	People's emotions
ana ni aruran	Are concentrated on a hole.
onna fumi	A woman's letter:
kashiko kashiko ni	"That's the place, that's it!"
kakisutete	Carelessly dashed off.

These examples can also be interpreted with quite innocuous meanings, but no doubt the indecent meanings suggested in the translation were intended. The *haikai* section in *Sōchō's Diary* includes examples of two different verses (*tsukeku*) added to the same *maeku* (previous verse) by Sōchō and Yamazaki Sōkan, the traditional founder of *haikai* poetry, clear evidence of the links between Sōchō and what would be the most typical poetry of the following centuries. Sōchō's fondness for unconventional poetry had still another side: he is credited with having compiled the collection of popular songs, *Kangin Shū*, in 1518.

From his poetry and what we know of his life Sōchō emerges as a distinctive personality, a poet who mastered the conventions of a rigorously demanding art only to break them.

ZEAMI

1333/4–1443

About forty years ago an abridged film version of the Nō play *Aoi no Ue* was made with the great actor Sakurama Kintarō. By present standards of film-making the photography is crude, but Sakurama's performance is superb. I have shown this film to my students many times,and each time I am greatly impressed by the actor's perfection of each gesture, each stamp of the foot. One drawback to the English version is the soundtrack explaining the action of the play and the art of Nō; it is atrocious. I cringe whenever I hear the voice say, "This primitive form of drama . . . . "

Primitive! Of the many forms of drama I have seen, Nō is undoubtedly the least primitive. Of course, it is hard to define the nature of primitiveness, but one can easily recognize primitive drama when one sees it. It is generally long, formless, and marked by a combination of extravagant posturing and extremely realistic (or even vulgar) elements. One can see such drama performed by adults in certain "unspoiled" parts of the world, and by middle-school students everywhere else. It is precisely the opposite of Nō.

Nō, in its present, highly evolved form, is unique among the theatrical arts of the world. Drama is usually discussed in terms of conflict, but in Nō conflict is rare because there is usually only one clearly defined person, the *shite*. He is in no sense in conflict with the *waki*, often a priest who merely asks the questions of the mysterious figure before him that the audience might ask. Some plays are devoted to describing the history of a shrine or to an event in the legendary past, without the least suggestion of conflict. Even when, on rare occasions, the *shite* and another character seem to be disagreeing briefly, this is generally not the central theme of the play.

Another common view of drama stresses the importance of the creation of memorable characters, but even the main "character" in Nō, the *shite*, has little personality, usually being no more than the incarnation of a powerful emotion—unforgiving enmity, possessive jealousy, remorse for an unspeakable deed, and so on.

Nor will it help our understanding of Nō if we attempt to consider it a kind of a form of drama in which the music inevitably takes precedence over the plot. The music is indeed a vital element in Nō, but it is inseparable from the words. A play may be admired for its story, its poetry or its dancing, but not for its music. Nobody ever whistles a favorite tune from Nō.

One can only conclude that Nō is unique. It is not easy to understand, but it pleases and moves audiences in a way not true of any other form of theatrical entertainment. Again and again people have predicted that Nō would soon disappear because of the changed tastes of the younger generations of Japanese, but today it flourishes as never before.

The beginnings of Nō, originally known as *sarugaku*, go back many centuries, but the form with which we are familiar today is essentially the work of one man, Zeami Motokiyo. His father, Kannami, was a famous Nō actor who also wrote some beautiful plays, most of which were later modified by Zeami to suit the more aristocratic tastes of his own age. Kannami's plays seem originally to have been more like drama in other countries, and they appealed even to audiences with little education because of their absorbing action, including conflicts. Kannami died in 1384 while performing in Suruga. By this time Zeami was no longer interested in appearing before unsophisticated audiences.

The special development of Nō came about due to an accident of history. In 1374, the Shogun Yoshimitsu, who was only seventeen, decided to attend a performance of Nō at the Imakumano Shrine in Kyoto. On that occasion Kannami appeared in the role of Okina, and his son, Zeami, appeared as Senzai in the play *Okina*. Yoshimitsu was so entranced by the performance that he bestowed his patronage on the troupe. Though young, he was a man of great culture and discrimination, and the plays written for his court were accordingly marked by complexity of language and thought that would not be understood by a poorly educated audience.

Zeami was only eleven when he was discovered by Yoshimitsu. Today eleven is considered too early an age for an actor to assume major Nō roles, but Zeami was of the belief, probably on the basis of his own experiences, that this was the age when a boy should begin mastering Nō repertory. He wrote, "A boy's childish appearance will give him charm, no matter what role he takes. At this age, his voice is also appealing. These two advantages will make people overlook his defects and will call attention to the development of his merits." Zeami went on to say that by the time a boy actor is sixteen, however, his voice changes and he loses the "flower" of his boyish beauty.

The emphasis Zeami placed on the beauty of boy actors reflects contemporary tastes at the court and in samurai circles. The role of Senzai, the role Zeami danced before Yoshimitsu, is still assigned to the handsomest actor of a company, who performs without a mask. We know how much Zeami attracted Yoshimitsu from the account written by a nobleman in 1378 which describes Yoshimitsu taking Zeami to see the Gion Festival. A special stand had been erected for the shogun to watch the procession passing down Shijō in Kyoto. "The shogun was accompanied by a boy, a Yamato *sarugaku* player, who watched the festival from the shogun's box. The shogun, who has for some time bestowed his affection on this boy, shared the same mat and passed him food from his own plate. These *sarugaku* performers are no better than beggars, but because this boy waits on the shogun and enjoys his esteem, everyone seeks his favor. Those who give the boy presents ingratiate themselves with the shogun. The daimyos and others vie to offer him gifts of enormous expense. A most distressing state of affairs."

Yoshimitsu was not the only important personage to show the boy affection. Nijō Yoshimoto (1320–88), a great nobleman who had several times served as regent and chancellor, was entranced by Zeami's precocious talents and good looks, and in 1375 he invited the boy to his mansion. Yoshimoto bestowed on the boy the name Fujiwaka, apparently taking the *fuji* from his own family name, Fujiwara. The boy later participated in *renga* parties with Yoshimoto and other masters, holding his own, despite his youth. His *tsukeku*, supplied to a *maeku* by Yoshimoto at a gathering in 1378, was pronounced "truly outstanding." The close relationship between the art of *renga* and of Nō is no doubt a product of Zeami's early associations with the techniques and spirit of *renga*, and is confirmed by the striking similarity in the vocabulary he used in discussing Nō to the vocabulary of *renga* criticism. Moreover, although both arts were colored by aristocratic preferences in literature—there are innumerable references to the imperial collections of *waka* poetry, *The Tale of Genji*, *The Tales of Ise*, and so on—the outstanding practitioners were commoners. Zeami was dismissed as a "beggar," but like Sōgi and Sōchō, the masters of *renga*, his talent brought him eminence.

Zeami was already an established actor when he succeeded his father as head of the troupe in 1384, but he seems to have fallen into a slump afterwards. In his book *Kadensho* (The Book of the Transmission of the Flower) he described in terms that suggest autobiography the ridicule which the public is likely to heap on an actor between the ages of seventeen and twenty-four, a period when his youthful beauty has disappeared but when his skills as a full-fledged actor have not yet emerged. During this critical period, the actor must summon all his determination to keep himself from abandoning Nō in despair.

Zeami apparently recovered from his depression during his middle twenties, when he achieved recognition as a truly outstanding performer. He wrote, "By this period the actor's voice has settled completely, and his body has assumed its adult proportions. . . . People begin to notice him and comment on his skill. . . . The public and the actor himself may then begin to think that he is truly accomplished, but this is most detrimental to the actor. His is not a true 'flower'; he is merely in the prime of his youth and the audience has been momentarily captivated by his charm." The actor, in order to avoid serious harm to his career, must not be deluded by flattery, but must study intently the techniques of older actors.

Zeami was in his middle thirties when he wrote *Kadensho*. He said that this age marked the culminating period in an actor's career. If he still has not won public recognition by then, he clearly does not possess a genuine "flower," and his performance will soon deteriorate. Zeami insisted on audience approval as the gauge of an actor's talents. The actor's function is to please the audience which alone will ultimately judge his merits. Zeami believed that the actor who has established a solid reputation by his middle thirties could preserve his "flower" even after he loses his physical beauty. A truly remarkable performer, like Kannami, who performed just a few weeks before his death in his fifty-second year, could still dazzle an audience, even though his repertory was drastically limited by his age. Zeami likened the talents of aged actors to flowers still blossoming on a withered tree.

In 1399, the year before he wrote *Kadensho*, Zeami appeared in festive performances of Nō which were attended for three days by Yoshimochi, the new shogun. The great success he scored on this occasion established his reputation as the leading *sarugaku* actor. It was the logical moment for him to take stock of his art. Zeami in his critical writings of this period revealed himself less as a theoretician of Nō than as a practical man of the theater who was concerned above all with winning the favor of his audiences.

The apogee of Zeami's career as an actor came in 1408 when he performed at Yoshimitsu's Kitayama mansion in the presence of the Emperor Go-Komatsu (the father of Ikkyū). A month later Yoshimitsu fell ill, and he died in his fifty-first year. This came as a severe blow to Zeami. Yoshimitsu had not only been a generous patron but was also the most discerning critic of Nō.

Yoshimochi bestowed his patronage especially on an actor named Zōami. Zeami was impressed by this actor and stated that he had been moved to tears by Zōami's "flower of stillness." But Yoshimochi's preference for Zōami seems to have caused Zeami to change the emphasis in his critical writings from Nō as performance to Nō as an aesthetic and literary art, as if he despaired of obtaining present success. In 1423 he wrote *Nōsakusho* (Book of Nō Composition), reflecting this new attitude. Undoubtedly, Zeami also wrote various Nō plays about the same time, but we cannot be sure which of his works date from this period.

In 1422 Zeami took orders as a Buddhist priest and left the position of head of the troupe to his elder son, Motomasa. Zeami had another son, Motoyoshi, for whom he wrote *Nōsakusho*. It has been suggested that this son probably wrote some of the plays traditionally attributed to Zeami whose authorship has since been questioned. Motoyoshi also recorded Zeami's opinions in *Sarugaku Dangi* (Lectures on *Sarugaku*; 1430), his most important work of criticism.

Motomasa quickly established a reputation as an outstanding actor following Zeami's tradition, and his future seemed assured when a threat arose unexpectedly in the person of Zeami's nephew, Motoshige. In 1428 Yoshimochi died without an heir and was therefore succeeded by his brother Yoshinori, who was hostile to both Zeami and Motomasa and was determined to establish Motoshige as the chief *sarugaku* actor. We can infer that Yoshinori's tastes were cruder than those of Yoshimitsu or Yoshimochi from the account of performances in 1429 at the Muromachi Palace when real horses were used, a far cry from Zeami's manner of stylized presentation. Ten days later Yoshinori forbade Zeami as well as Motomasa to perform before the Retired Emperor. Yoshinori's persecution became so severe that in 1430 Motomasa went to perform in a remote part of Yamato, and Motoyoshi gave up the theater to become a Buddhist priest. Yoshinori's preference for realism and action, as opposed to Zeami's *yūgen* (mysterious beauty), became the trend in the Muromachi period, and only in the seventeenth century was Zeami's position as the supreme figure in Nō again recognized.

In 1432 Zeami suffered a terrible blow with Motomasa's death as we know from his account, *Museki Isshi*. He experienced further disaster when in 1434 he was banished to the island of Sado. We do not know why Yoshinori exiled Zeami, but his hatred must have been implacable for him to have sent a man in his seventies into lonely exile. Zeami probably remained on Sado until 1441, when a general amnesty was declared after the assassination of Yoshinori, who was killed while watching a performance of *sarugaku*. After Zeami's return to Kyoto he lived with his son-in-law and successor as head of his school, Komparu Zenchiku, until his death in 1443.

The personality of Zeami does not emerge as vividly as that of the more eccentric artists of his time, yet we can sense in many plays the powerful emotions of a man who led a most extraordinary life. He expressed these emotions not only in the indirect, subdued manner of the *waka* poets but often with overt power. In his masterpiece, *Kinuta*, the *shite*, incensed by her husband's failure to return, sends for a *kinuta* (fulling block) on which to pound out her grief:

inga no mōshū	Tears of remembrance
omoi no namida	For sins committed
kinuta ni kakareba	Fall on the fulling block;
namida wa kaette	The tears turn to flames,
kaen to natte	And choked by the smoke
mune no kemuri no	Of the fire in my breast,
honō ni musebeba	I shriek, but my voice
sakedo koe ga	Does not escape my lips.
ideba koso	The fulling block is soundless,
kinuta mo koe naku	The pine wind too, unheard—
matsukaze mo kikoezu	Only the shouts of hell's
kashaku no koe no mi	tormentors,
osoroshiya	Horrible their cries!

The imagery is overpowering—tears that turn to flames, mute shrieks of anguish, the cries of the fiends of hell—and gives the play its intense dramatic effect. I doubt that Japanese poetry can be more powerful. Zeami ranks as one of the greatest Japanese poets as well as the greatest dramatist and the greatest critic of the theater.

Zeami's plays are absolute. They are as much about our time as about the Muromachi period. However, their particular expression is the product of the special atmosphere to which he was introduced as a child. Zeami was an exception among Nō playwrights because of his emphasis on *yūgen*, a standard of beauty rare in the theaters of the world. Far from being primitive, his Nō plays go beyond the drama of other countries in the way they manage to express with the greatest economy of means the most profound emotions.

A gate of the Tōfuku-ji, site of Shōtetsu's tomb

SHŌTETSU

1381–1475

Most experts are agreed that the Muromachi period had little to offer in the way of *waka*. Even those who grudgingly express some admiration for the *waka* in the two imperially sponsored anthologies *Gyokuyōshū* (Jade Leaves Collection; 1312) and *Fūgashū* (Collection of Graceful Poems; 1346), usually dismiss the poetry of later men as "uncreative." In truth, it is difficult for an outsider to approach the *waka* of this period. When I read the accounts of the bitter quarrels between the adherents of the conservative Nijō school and the more innovative Reizei school, the matters that seemed so crucial to poets of these schools strike me as being drearily inconsequential. At our distance from the period discussions of the various faults of poetry listed in the books of *waka* theory, or the exact pedigree of the different masters of the *waka*, can hardly hold our attention very long.

But the *waka* of the Muromachi period was not unrelated to the other, more famous, literary arts of the time, and the work of one poet in particular, Shōtetsu, is of exceptional interest, not only because of the intrinsic quality of his *waka*, but because he helped to formulate aesthetic ideals that are still valid today.

Shōtetsu was born in the province of Bitchū, the second son of a provincial official. At an early age he was ordained as a Buddhist priest and entered the Tōfuku-ji, one of the five great Zen temples of Kyoto. Even as a small child he had shown aptitude at *waka* composition. A passage in his book of criticism, *Shōtetsu Monogatari* (compiled about 1450), describes how as a boy he wrote *waka* on leaves for the Tanabata Festival. There must have been other occasions when he displayed precocious talent, for when he was only fourteen he was invited by a priest to visit an elderly magistrate who lived nearby in Kyoto and who was known as a lover of poetry. After some hesitation the boy accepted the invitation. Here is Shōtetsu's account of what happened.

"The Lay Priest Jibu, at the time a venerable gentleman over eighty years of age with white hair, came out to meet us. He said, 'These days one never hears anything about children writing poetry, but when I was young it used to be quite common. How charming of you! I have a poetry gathering every month on the twenty-fifth. Please do attend. Here are the subjects for this month.' So saying, he himself wrote down the topics for me. There were three, each written with four Chinese characters: the quiet moon late at night, distant geese over mountains at twilight, and a love affair not followed by a letter after parting. This took place at the beginning of the eighth month.

"On the twenty-fifth I went to attend the meeting. Inside the house, Reizei no Tametada and Reizei no Tamekuni sat in one place of honor, and the former governor of Kyushu in the other. Behind them were their close retainers and my host's family, over twenty persons in all, seated impressively in rows. I had arrived

late, so I was shown to the central place of honor.[1] This was how
I made my entrance, precipitous though it was. The governor
was at the time a lay priest, over eighty years old, and he sat there
wearing a robe without the usual black hems and a sash with a
long tassel.

"My poem on the topic 'quiet moon late at night' was:

itazura ni	How light the sky is
fukeyuku sora no	This night as, to no avail,
kage nare ya	It grows ever later—
hitori nagamuru	All alone I stare up at
aki no yo no tsuki	The moon of an autumn night.

"My poem on the wild geese concluded, as I recall:

yama no ha ni	At the mountain edge
hitotsura miyuru	A whole chain is visible—
hatsukari no koe	The voices of the first wild geese.

"I have forgotten the first part of the poem. I do not remember
my poem on love either.

"As the result of frequent appearances at such sessions, I learned
how to compose poetry. I was fourteen years old at the time.[2]
Afterwards, while I was in the service of the resident prince at
Nara, I was the senior page whenever memorial services were
conducted in the Lecture Hall on Mount Hiei. I was so busy with
these and other duties that I stopped writing poetry for a time.
Later, after my father died,[3] I again made so bold as to appear
at poetry gatherings and resumed my composition. I filled thirty-
six notebooks with poems composed from the time of the
meeting at Jibu's place. There must have been over twenty thousand poems. They were all burnt at Imakumano.[4] I have composed somewhat under ten thousand poems since then."

Shōtetsu's surviving *waka*, over eleven thousand in all, are
contained in *Sōkon Shū* (Grass Roots Collection; 1459). He was

not only an unusually prolific poet, but was also well-versed in *The Tale of Genji* and other classics. His criticism of *waka*, both of his own time and of much earlier, is exceptionally acute.

Shōtetsu's training in *waka* seems to have come mainly from the former governor of Kyushu, Imagawa Ryōshun (1325–1420), whom he first met at the house of the magistrate. Although Ryōshun was active as a soldier in an era of constant warfare, he had set his heart on becoming a poet ever since he was fifteen, when he saw in a dream the twelfth-century poet Minamoto Tsunenobu. Tsunenobu was known as a poetic innovator, and that may be why Ryōshun chose to follow the style of the "radical" Reizei school, rather than the prevalent Nijō school. One *waka* by Ryōshun was included in *Fūgashū*, an imperial anthology produced by the Reizei school during the brief period it was favored by the court. But Ryōshun, in his capacity as commanding general in Kyushu, was far too busy with military duties to spare much time for poetry. He returned to Kyoto when he was about seventy and only then began his literary career.

Ryōshun's works of criticism, which were written mainly between his seventy-sixth and eighty-seventh years, advocated greater freedom of poetic language than had hitherto been tolerated. It had been the practice to restrict the *waka* to words found in the celebrated collection *Kokinshū*, compiled some five hundred years earlier, but Ryōshun denied that new words were objectionable. He wrote, "Even if a new word is used for the first time, why should one avoid it, providing it does not fall unpleasantly on the ears?" He also favored straightforward expression. He wrote, with the philosophy of a blunt military man, "The essence of poetry is describing things just as they are, without decoration." His most famous statement on poetry was to the effect that any expression which comes directly from the heart is poetry. "If it is cold and one says, 'I wish I had a cloak to wear,' that is poetry, and if one says, 'I wish I could warm myself by the fire,' that is also poetry."

Such simple, uncomplicated language was certainly not typical of the expression of the *waka* as it has evolved during the centuries since the *Kokinshū*. It indicated an impatience with the trivial controversies over poetic diction that were so common in poetic circles of the day. A poem that says nothing more than "I wish I could warm myself by the fire" is obviously not very interesting, even if it comes from the heart; what makes Ryōshun's argument intriguing is that it is so unlike the elaborate discussions of *waka* in other books of poetic criticism. Shōtetsu was influenced by Ryōshun's insistence on unhackneyed expression, but he was even more influenced by Ryōshun's indifference to the factional disputes that separated the Nijō and Reizei schools. Although Shōtetsu acknowledged that he had been influenced by Ryōshun, he claimed that he drew his poetic inspiration directly from Fujiwara Teika, whom he venerated above all other poets. Shōtetsu denied that belonging to a particular school made much difference. He privately said to his favorite disciple, the *renga* poet Shinkei, "I have no affection for either the Nijō or the Reizei schools, which are sadly degenerated offsprings of the Master's teachings." He also told Shinkei, "I realize that I am the outstanding exponent of the Reizei school, but I find the matter of schools very tedious. I learn only from what lies in the hearts of Shunzei and Teika." In public Shōtetsu was sometimes obliged to declare his affiliations with the Reizei traditions, but at heart he remained an iconoclast, who worshiped only one god, Teika. His book of poetic criticism, *Shōtetsu Monogatari*, opens with the prediction, "Those who, though they practice the way of poetry, look down on Teika will not enjoy the blessings of providence, but will suffer punishment." On another occasion he stated, "I intend to end my days as a believer in the Teika sect." Like the *kogiha* (Ancient Meaning school) Confucian philosophers of the Tokugawa period who insisted on going directly back to the *Analects*, rather than allow themselves to be led astray by later commentaries, Shōtetsu returned to Teika as the fountainhead of wisdom about the *waka*, rejecting the many secret traditions that had been fostered by the rival schools. This intransigence, more than any other aspect of poetic tradition, is what Shōtetsu seems to have learned from Ryōshun.

But Shōtetsu, unlike Ryōshun, was not satisfied with expressing directly what he felt in his heart; he was not only an excellent poet but a critic who could explain and analyze his poetry. Here is his *waka* on the subject of "falling blossoms," together with his commentary:

> "sakeba chiru
> yo no ma no hana no
> yume no uchini
> yagate magirenu
> mine no shirakumo

> They blossomed but to fall
> In the space of but one night,
> Blossoms within a dream;
> But then I saw they had not
>   vanished—
> The white clouds on the
>   mountain.

"This is a poem in the *yūgen* style. What we call *yūgen* is something within the mind which cannot be expressed in words. The quality of *yūgen* may be suggested by the sight of a thin cloud veiling the moon or by autumn mist swathing the scarlet leaves on a mountainside. If one is asked where the *yūgen* in these sights lies, one cannot answer, and it is not surprising that a man who fails to understand this truth is likely to prefer the sight of the moon shining brightly in a cloudless sky. It is quite impossible to explain wherein lies the interest or wonder of *yūgen*.

"The words 'within a dream; But then I saw they had not vanished' come from a poem recited by Genji. Genji, on meeting Fujitsubo, composed the poem

> mite mo mata
> au yo mare naru
> yume no uchi ni
> yagate magiruru

> We met, but when again?
> How rare will be our nights
>   together.
> If only within a dream

ukimi to mo gana	I might vanish as I am—
	Such is my sad destiny.

It too was in the *yūgen* style."

Shōtetsu's remarks about the nature of *yūgen* are among the most persuasive ever made. In Zeami's writings *yūgen* usually meant elegance, the quality he associated with the speech and behavior of the nobility, but Shōtetsu was describing something closer to what Europeans of four hundred years later would call symbolism. In the confused, dark days of the fifteenth century it was perhaps not too surprising that Shōtetsu preferred a veiled, remote beauty to the obvious charms of nature, and if someone denied that his *yūgen* was anything more than the "emperor's new clothes," he did not think it was worth arguing about.

This preference for suggestion, for mystery, expressed itself in the poetic arts influenced by Zen. Shōtetsu's disciple Shinkei wrote, "In *waka* and *renga* there must be both Zen and Buddhist doctrine." Shōtetsu wrote many religious poems, some specifically of Zen inspiration like the following:

tera wa aredo	There is a temple,
mukashi no mama no	But is has become a Buddha
kazari naki	Without ornaments,
hotoke to narite	As Buddha was long ago—
yama zo aseyuku	The mountain loses color.

This poem, written in 1452 when Shōtetsu was seventy-one, is a difficult but characteristic expression of Zen beliefs. The temple exists and Shōtetsu has sat there in meditation, but the temple itself is not of importance. The achievement of Buddhahood is the reason for the temple's existence, and the mountain on which the temple stands, gradually losing color and shape in the dusk, has itself attained the eternal essence of Buddhahood, free of worldly adornment. Despite Shōtetsu's great respect for the past, evinced not only by his unqualified admiration of Teika but by his allusions to *The Tale of Genji* (as above), his Zen beliefs establish him as a contemporary of Ikkyū and other priest-poets of his time.

Shōtetsu is the last major figure in Muromachi *waka* poetry. Not for many years—perhaps, it might be argued, never again—would the *waka*, the most ancient Japanese poetic form, serve as the vehicle for the finest poetic expression of an age. Its place was taken in successive periods by *renga*, the *haiku*, and poetry in the modern style. However, despite his eminence as the outstanding *waka* poet of his time, Shōtetsu was for a long time not shown proper recognition. Apart from the agony of losing all his poems in a fire, he suffered ill treatment at the hands of the shogun, Ashikaga Yoshinori (1394–1441), who hated the Reizei school and everyone associated with it. Yoshinori ordered Shōtetsu's lands to be confiscated, and when an imperially sponsored anthology was compiled in 1439, he saw to it that not one poem by Shōtetsu was included, though he was undoubtedly the best *waka* poet of the day. It is ironic that Shōtetsu, who expressed such disdain for the partisanship of members of different schools of poetry, should have suffered so greatly because of his nominal affiliation with the Reizei school.

In 1441, after the assassination of Yoshinori, both the Reizei school and Shōtetsu came into favor. Many pupils sought his guidance, including military men such as Hosokawa Katsumoto. However, his most important pupil was Shinkei, who in turn became the teacher of Sōgi; Shōtetsu's influence was thus stronger on *renga* than on *waka*, and many characteristic features of *renga* style and mood were ultimately derived from Shōtetsu.

Today Shōtetsu is relatively little remembered, yet he belonged to a small but extraordinary group of Muromachi figures who formed Japanese aesthetic tastes for centuries to come. Like Ikkyū, he was impatient with formal restrictions; like Sōgi and Sōchō, he was moved as much by the unspoken thoughts and associations in a man's mind as by the conventionally admired sights of nature; and like Zeami, he sought to go beyond appearances to ultimate truths. Like all of them, he created works of beauty that were at once personal and for all time.

NOTES

1. Presumably, everyone else was too diffident to sit in the *yokoza*, so the place was empty until Shōtetsu arrived.
2. By Japanese reckoning: thirteen by Western count.
3. In 1403, when Shōtetsu was twenty-two.
4. Imakumano was in the southern part of Kyoto. The fire occurred in 1432.

THE SIXTEENTH CENTURY

Most of the sixteenth century was given over to warfare. The first half of this century is often referred to as the period of *geko-kujō*, a term meaning that those below overthrew their superiors. Innumerable petty rulers won battles only to be eventually defeated by their own subordinates. This part of the century is also known as Sengoku, a name borrowed from Chinese history but used to mean "country at war" rather than "warring states."

In the early 1540s Portuguese soldiers and priests made their way to Japan, opening the first direct contact between Japan and Europe. They introduced firearms and religion; in 1549 St. Francis Xavier landed in the southern port of Kagoshima, and in the following year preached at various places, including the capital. Christianity spread among the people, especially in areas where the Portuguese had preached.

In the meantime the country was being brought under the control of one man, Oda Nobunaga (1534–1582), a general from the province of Owari whose military ability brought him victory over many adversaries, including at times some of the Ashikaga shoguns. In 1568 Nobunaga entered Kyoto along with a member of the Ashikaga family whom he had chosen to be the shogun. Some scholars consider that this event marked the end of the Sengoku period, but there was much fighting to be done before unification of the country became a reality. Nobunaga, who hated the Buddhist monks, especially those with military power, favored the Christians, and in 1576, when he established his headquarters at Azuchi, on the shores of Lake Biwa, he allowed the Portuguese missionaries to build a church in the city.

Nobunaga was a fierce and ruthless man, but he resembled other Japanese generals in his eagerness to acquire culture. He patronized the Nō theater and was able to compose linked verse, after a fashion. Nobunaga was killed in 1582 by a rival general. Unification of Japan was achieved by Toyotomi Hideyoshi (1536–1598), a general who had served under Nobunaga and who had avenged Nobunaga's death by killing the assassin. Hideyoshi was even more determined than Nobunaga to be considered a cultured man. He not only enjoyed watching Nō but performed even the most difficult roles, and he showed special interest in the tea ceremony. In 1587 Hideyoshi completed the unification of Japan begun by Nobunaga. Unlike military men of former times who had claimed the office of shogun after establishing their supremacy, Hideyoshi, in keeping with his professed admiration for the old Japanese traditions, had himself named *kampaku*, or chancellor, in the manner of the great nobles of five hundred or more years earlier.

Initially Hideyoshi had been intrigued by the Europeans, but in 1589 he issued a first decree prohibiting Christianity. This did not prevent fashionable young men of the time from ordering European clothes from Nagasaki. Despite the anti-Christian edicts, moreover, many young men and women sported crucifixes, not out of religious conviction but to be abreast of the latest vogue.

In 1596 Hideyoshi, having been informed that Christian religious activity in Japan was intended to promote the conquest of the country by the king of Spain, ordered the arrest of twenty-six Spanish priests and converts in Kyoto. They were taken to Nagasaki where they were crucified in 1597. Hideyoshi died in 1598. Two years later the Battle of Sekigahara was fought between those loyal to Hideyoshi's family and supporters of Tokugawa Ieyasu (1542–1616). The victory of the Tokugawa forces brought an end to the cosmopolitan culture associated with Hideyoshi's name. Tokugawa Ieyasu took over authority and founded the shogunate, a military regime that lasted until 1867.

The Hokuendō at Kōfuku-ji

SATOMURA JŌHA

1524–1602

As far as literature is concerned, the Sengoku period was a period characterized by beginnings and ends rather than of fruition. The incessant warfare, starting with the Ōnin War in 1467, drove the writers of traditional literature from the capital to the countryside to seek refuge with local potentates. This had the desirable result of the traditional culture being spread to many distant regions, but there was no longer any one center where men could come together to create *waka*, *renga*, or *kanshi*. Eventually, as order was temporarily restored, the poets began to drift back to the capital, but by this time the great figures of the past were dead. Perhaps that is why so many new literary arts germinated in this period.

Among the literary arts which met their ends during the Sengoku period, none was more conspicuous than *renga*. It was the chief poetic art of the period and surely none of the *renga* poets dreamt that their art was dying, but few scholars today can name even one poet of serious *renga* from the Tokugawa period. Comic *renga*, it is true, persisted into the nineteenth century, but the art that was perfected by such men as Nijō Yoshimoto, Sōgi, and Sōchō died with Satomura Jōha, the last of the *renga* masters.

Jōha was probably the outstanding literary figure of the Sengoku period. His poetry has been forgotten, but his career is of special interest because of the light it sheds on the fate of artists in a violently changing society.

Jōha was born in 1524 in Nara, the son of a temple servant at the Ichijō-in, a temple of the Hossō sect. The occupation was a humble one, but it was probably not without influence. Jōha received a good education, and even after the death of his father, when he was only twelve, he did not experience financial hardship. Nevertheless, he knew that as a younger son he would have to make a career for himself to live. In later years Jōha told his disciple Matsunaga Teitoku why he eventually decided to become a *renga* master. He said, "A man who fails to make a name for himself before he is thirty will never succeed in life. I examined my prospects carefully, and it seemed to me that becoming a *renga* master would be an easy way to get ahead. After all, at *renga* gatherings even artisans and townsmen sit side by side with members of the nobility."

Jōha was ordained as a priest in 1542, but instead of remaining in a temple he went to Kyoto to study *renga*. Perhaps he thought being a priest would be something to fall back on if he failed as a poet. In any case, *renga* masters normally shaved their heads and dressed like priests. His first teacher, Shūkei, died only two years after Jōha became his pupil, and his next teacher, Satomura Shōkyū, died seven years later. For Jōha the deaths of these teachers were misfortunes, but they enabled him to rise automatically in the hierarchy of *renga* masters. Although Jōha had gradually built up a reputation as a promising young poet, it took a long time to gain recognition, and sometimes he thought of giving up *renga* altogether. With the death of Shōkyū in 1542, however, Jōha succeeded as head of the Satomura school. Only one man, Tani Sōyō, ranked higher than he. Although Sōyō was younger than Jōha, he had the advantage of being born into a celebrated family of *renga* poets, and he was more talented than Jōha.

As the head of the Satomura school Jōha was permitted to participate in poetry gatherings of the nobility; his dream of sitting side by side with men of high birth had been realized. He made his living by teaching *renga* composition, chiefly to members of the military class who wished to acquire culture.

At this time the nobles were hard-pressed financially because of the loss of their estates, and they had almost no political power, but they were still respected for their ancestry and because they were the repositories of the old traditions. Jōha became intimate with members of the Konoe and Sanjōnishi families. In the spring of 1553, when Sanjōnishi Kin'eda journeyed to Yoshino to admire the cherry blossoms, he took Jōha along. The country was in disorder and Kin'eda was suffering real financial hardships, but he was a pillar of the old court culture, and Jōha was delighted to travel with such a man. The most interesting feature of Kin'eda's *Yoshino Mōde no Ki* (A Visit to Yoshino) which consists mainly of descriptions of places mentioned in poetry, is the unspoken fact that Jōha, the son of a temple servant, was associating familiarly with a great noble despite the differences in their social position and age. Jōha had chosen the right profession, for only the mastery of an artistic skill could have enabled him to rise so conspicuously.

Jōha was not yet especially accomplished as a poet, but he attracted various important patrons, and their support enabled him to live comfortably. His most important patron was Miyoshi Chōkei who, despite his sometimes ferocious behavior, was fond of literature, especially *renga*, and did much to advance Jōha's career.

In 1563 Sanjōnishi Kin'eda died at the age of seventy-six. The grief-stricken Jōha composed a thousand-link solitary *renga* in honor of his late mentor and friend. It begins:

toshigoto no	How bitter to think
hana naranu yo no	The world is without him,
urami kana	though flowers
furinishi ato mo	Blossom every year.
niwa no harukusa	Even amidst the old remains,
yama no ha no	Spring grasses in the garden.
usuyuki nokoru	I can see the dew,
tsuyu miete	All that lingers of the thin snow
	That lay on the mountain edge.

This solitary *renga* was probably his finest work, and the elegiac tone conveys feelings much deeper than Jōha's earlier poetry.

In the same year a son of Miyoshi Chōkei's was poisoned, allegedly by Matsunaga Hisahide, another patron of Jōha. No doubt this tragedy affected Jōha in that it stirred fresh thoughts on the uncertainty of life in so turbulent a society. But the most important event of this year for Jōha was the death of Tani Sōyō at the early age of thirty-seven. Thanks to this death, Jōha was now the sole figure at the apex of the hierarchy of *renga* poets.

Jōha led a busy life in the capital. His special influence both with the nobles and the military led to his being approached by dignitaries from the provinces who wished to be invited to poetry gatherings held by the great men, and no doubt they paid Jōha handsomely for his intercession. He was not the only one to trade his literary influence for financial rewards. The nobles, who had fallen on hard days, gratefully accepted gifts from even the most boorish daimyos and copied out classical texts for the visitors to take home as souvenirs of the capital. Jōha felt no hesitation about serving as a kind of pander to the nobles longing to sell the aura of their names to rich bumpkins attracted by the old culture. His income was derived, however, mainly from the correction fees he charged amateurs who sought his guidance. A wealthy amateur would submit samples of his *renga* to the master, who changed a word here and there, imparting grace to an uncertain composition. Jōha's fees were apparently high, and he led a life of luxury that in no way resembled the austere existence of the hermit-priests of the Middle Ages. Far from taking refuge in a hut deep in the mountains, he lived in the city, surrounded by admirers.

1567 was a year of desperate fighting. The countryside was torn by warfare, and in the capital there was no central authority. This was the year Jōha chose to fulfill his cherished dream of visiting Mount Fuji. He was on the road for over six months, but his journal rarely indicates that he was traveling through a war-torn country. One affecting passage describes his visit to the lonely hut where the *renga* master Sōchō had lived forty or fifty years earlier. The atmosphere of the journal is prevailingly cheerful, but Jōha's account mentioned how he was forced to turn back when Oda Nobunaga's army was attacking the castle of Nagashima which was held by the Ikkō sect. Even while the most desperate fighting was going on at Nagashima, Jōha was lavishly entertained at a nearby town. He wrote, "Sometime after midnight I happened to look to the west, and I saw that the castle at Nagashima had been taken and many fires had been set. The light was bright as day, so I rose from my bed." He composed this *waka*:

tabi makura	A traveler's pillow—
yumeji tanomu ni	I had set forth on a path of
aki no yo no	dreams,
tsuki ni akasan	But now I shall spend
matsukaze no sato	This night of autumn moonlight
	In a village of pine winds.

There is certainly something inadequate in this conventional poem, and unless the reader knows the background, he would hardly guess the circumstances.

In 1568 Oda Nobunaga entered Kyoto. When the fighting died down and it was apparent that Nobunaga was the master of the capital, Jōha was among the first to offer his congratulations. Reports had spread through the capital that Nobunaga was a monster "more terrifying than any demon," and people trembled with fear at the horrid fate awaiting them. But Jōha hurried to the Tōfuku-ji, Nobunaga's headquarters, and offered him a pair of fans with these verses:

nihon te ni iru   Oh, the joy I feel today
kyō no yorokobi   You take these two fans in hand.

The point of these lines is the pun on *nihon*, meaning "two (fans)" and "Japan." Jōha was no doubt seeking to ingratiate himself with the conqueror. Nobunaga, although he was not a literary man, replied:

maiasobu   These are fans
chiyo yorozuyo   For joyous dance of a thousand,
ōgi ni te   Ten thousand ages.

This unexpected skill at *renga* displayed by Nobunaga was quickly reported throughout the capital. "Old and young, learning of this, were speechless with astonishment. They had supposed that because this man was a fierce warrior things would be the same as when Kiso no Yoshinaka burst into the capital long ago, but Nobunaga seemed to be gentle and refined. People were relieved at the thought that things were likely to go easily, and they all breathed a sigh of relief." (From *Shinchō Ki*).

Surely the political and social functions of *renga* had never been more conspicuously displayed! Jōha's importance as a spokesman for the traditional culture was apparent from this incident. About this time he also became friendly with Akechi Mitsuhide, who was a devoted amateur poet of *renga*. A few days before Mitsuhide

assassinated Nobunaga in 1582, he had joined in a *renga* session
with Jōha and other poets, ostensibly to pray for victory in an
attack against the Mōri family. *Renga* was believed to possess the
power to move the gods to grant victory in warfare, and Mitsuhide may have desired such assistance when he contemplated the
assassination. He opened the session with the verse:

toki wa ima	Now is the time
ame ga shita shiru	To rule 'all under heaven'—
satsuki kana	It's the fifth moon!

The point of the verse was the pun on *toki*, meaning time, but also
Toki, the clan-name of Mitsuhide's family. The poem plainly
revealed Mitsuhide's ambitions of taking control of the country.
Jōha was alarmed at the thought that he might be implicated.
After the assassination he was in fact interrogated by Toyotomi
Hideyoshi, but he managed to convince him of his innocence. In
fact, under Hideyoshi he rose from being a *renga* master to the
status of an adviser on all cultural matters.

Although Jōha benefited from the patronage of the military
leaders, he never took sides. He saw nothing strange about partic-
ipating in *renga* sessions held by enemies, even when the purpose
of these sessions was to secure victory in war. He wrote his most
important work of *renga* theory, *Renga Shihōshō*, at the request of
Akechi Mitsuhide, but presented it on completion to Mitsuhide's
enemy Hideyoshi, along with a fulsome postface acclaiming the
new master of Japan.

Jōha was friendly not only with Hideyoshi but with his nephew
Hidetsugi, the celebrated "murderous chancellor." When Hidetsugi fell from Hideyoshi's favor and was ordered to commit suicide, Jōha was banished. This was the first instance of bad luck in
Jōha's whole life, and it must have surprised him. There was no
way to resist, but Jōha did not contemplate suicide. He lived at the
Mii-dera until he was pardoned by Hideyoshi in 1597.

Jōha, the master of survival, outlived Hideyoshi by four years, and died in 1602. I should like to think of him serving Tokugawa Ieyasu in his last years, but I have seen no clear evidence to this effect. In any case, there cannot have been many men who successfully served Nobunaga, Mitsuhide, Hideyoshi, and Hidetsugi in an age of sudden deaths.

Jōha died in Nara, at his brother's house. For a time his death went unnoticed in the capital, but when the Daimyo Hosokawa Yūsai heard about it, a look of grief passed over his face. He said, "We'll never see his likes again."

ŌMURA YŪKO

1536–1596

In times of disorder the most prudent course for any man is to remain inconspicuous. Nevertheless, men of talent, whether inspired by a belief in the leader of some new movement, or merely desiring to profit by the ease of advancement in an unstable situation, have frequently placed their art at the service of a tyrant. Generally they are unable to realize that the seemingly all-powerful man they serve is doomed to fall from power one day; but sometimes, even when they expect that the tyrant will not last forever, they feel confident that they can successfully explain their actions to his successor. It is possible to cite fairly recent examples, such as the well-known French writers and musicians who collaborated with the Nazis during the occupation of France, or the Dutch scholar who dedicated volumes of his translation of the *Manyōshū* to Mussolini and Hitler.

In the Sengoku period (1524–1602) it was difficult for an intellectual not to become involved in the constant struggles for power. Many Japanese military men (unlike military men in most other countries) prided themselves on their literary and artistic abilities, and they eagerly sought to attract to their houses experts who could improve their own poetic compositions and who would flatter them by praising even the most incompetent efforts. Hitler began his career as a painter, but painting did not play a major role in his life once he became the master of the German state. Hideyoshi, on the other hand, continued to the end to write *renga* and to perform in Nō, as if to prove that he was really following the traditions of the chancellors (*kampaku*) of the Heian period, who were men not only of authority but of culture.

Hideyoshi attracted to his court most of the outstanding men of culture of his day. Some must have found it distasteful to serve him. It certainly must have offended the famous tea master Sen no Rikyū to perform his tea ceremony in the hut of solid gold that Hideyoshi built; and in the end, like many others who have temporarily enjoyed the patronage of tyrants, he was forced to kill himself. Other men, like Satomura Jōha, survived by writing a poetry that was so ambiguous that it did not definitely associate him with any one ruler. Ōmura Yūko, on the other hand, was a sycophant, who devoted his great talent to praising Hideyoshi. The fact that he is so little remembered today suggests the dangers to a man's reputation if he chooses the quick way to fame by currying favor with a tyrant.

Ōmura Yūko was born in 1536, the same year as Hideyoshi, in the province of Banshū. Apparently he did not come from an especially distinguished family. That may have been why he was sent to Kyoto to study at the Shōkoku-ji under the Zen master Ninjo Shūgyō. A fellow pupil at this time was Matsunaga Eishu, the father of Teitoku; the two became life-long friends. In later years, Yūko even tried to adopt Teitoku; no doubt Yūko would be more widely remembered today if Eishu had not refused. While at the Shōkoku-ji, Yūko studied not only the Buddhist sutras but also *waka, renga,* and the Japanese classics. He was so proficient that he eventually became known as the foremost scholar of non-Buddhist literature. He learned to write Chinese prose and poetry skillfully, as we know from his later works.

It is not clear when Yūko first met Hideyoshi. Perhaps it was in 1578, when Hideyoshi, who was about to attack Yūko's native place, Miki, in Banshū, asked him to come along as the official chronicler. Hideyoshi was only one of various generals serving under Nobunaga, but evidently he had a keen sense of his historical importance. Yūko's account of the siege of Miki Castle, *Banshū Go Seibatsu no koto* (The Conquest of Banshū), opens with a description of how warfare happened to break out in 1578 between Hideyoshi's army and that of the youthful Bessho Nagaharu, the lord of Miki Castle. This account, little known because it is written in Chinese, is quite as moving as more famous examples of war tales. The most impressive section occurs towards the end when, after two years of siege, provisions in the castle were exhausted and the defenders could not resist any longer. On January 15, 1580, a messenger arrived in Hideyoshi's camp with a letter of petition from the defenders. Nagaharu, his younger brother Tomoyuki, and his uncle, the governor of Yamashiro, agreed to commit *seppuku* on the seventeenth at *shinkoku* (between 4 and 6 p.m.) But, they added, it would be a pity if their soldiers would also have to die, so they asked that their lives be spared. Surely this must be one of the rare documents from the Sengoku period which reveals such humanistic sentiments. Hideyoshi, moved by the petition, agreed to spare the soldiers' lives, and he further expressed his admiration by sending several casks of saké to Nagaharu.

Nagaharu and his brother Tomoyuki spent the next two nights drinking with their families, but on the morning of the seventeenth the brothers rose early, bathed, and perfumed themselves. They sent a message to their uncle reminding him of the promise to commit suicide that afternoon. The uncle replied that it would be foolish to spare the soldiers' lives, and urged the brothers instead to burn the castle and perish in the flames together with the soldiers. The soldiers, learning of this, were infuriated. They dragged out the governor of Yamashiro and cut off his head. Nagaharu commented, "It has been my resolve all along to die. Now the last moments of my family have come." First he placed his three-year-old child on his lap and, after stroking the child's hair, stabbed him through the chest. Next he took his wife in his arms and, lying beside her on the same pillow, killed her, then covered her with a silken cloth. Tomoyuki killed his wife in the same way. Then the two brothers, taking each other's hand, sat side by side on a single *tatami* and composedly prepared for death. Nagaharu recalled the long days of the siege and bitterly regretted they had been to no avail. "However," he added, there could be no greater joy than that by our deaths we will save the lives of our soldiers." The two brothers then committed *seppuku*. Nagaharu was twenty-three and Tomoyuki twenty-one. Their uncle's wife, more faithful than her husband to his promise, killed her three children and then herself. Yūko reported, "Everyone who saw or heard of these events wetted his sleeves with tears of grief." The next day, in keeping with the agreement, the soldiers of the castle all came out unharmed. One of them, a page, brought several *tanzaku* (poem slips) on which were written the farewell poems of Nagaharu, his wife, Tomoyuki, Tomoyuki's wife, and others. Nagaharu's poem was:

ima wa tada	Now I feel no trace
urami mo arazu	Even of resentment
morobito no	When I realize
inochi ni kawaru	That I sacrifice my life
wagami to omoeba	To save those of many men.

His wife's poem was equally impressive:

morotomo ni	How happy I am
kiehatsuru koso	We shall vanish together
ureshikere	At the same time
okure sakidatsu	In this world where usually
narai naru yo wo	One dies first, the other later.

The account concludes with an enumeration of other victories by Hideyoshi and with a list of his ten great virtues. Yūko's final words were, "This truly was a man who stood out from the common herd. He is indeed worthy of our admiration. He is the foundation of the long prosperity of the shogun's house. This is a matter for great rejoicing."

This, the first of Yūko's accounts of Hideyoshi's exploits, proves that he was a writer of unusual ability. *Tenshōki*, the name by which the whole series of war accounts is known, is without a doubt a neglected masterpiece. But the importance of this work was not only literary. It proclaimed, apparently with sincerity, Yūko's great admiration for Hideyoshi, which was to be rewarded. Two years later he was appointed the steward of the Temman Shrine in Osaka, a position he retained to his death. When Hideyoshi became the ruler of Japan in 1582, Yūko was a central figure in his inner circle of *otogishu*, entertainers and advisers on cultural matters. No doubt Yūko at times had to endure humiliation, but for fifteen years he never lost Hideyoshi's confidence. He wrote not only eyewitness accounts of Hideyoshi's campaigns, accompanying him even to Kyushu, but also did pieces celebrating the recovery of Hideyoshi's mother from illness or the birth of his son Tsurumatsu. This was expected of an *otogishu*.

There is a description of Yūko written in 1591: "He is withered in his appearance and aged in his spirit; he is clumsy in speech but eloquent with his brush." Despite his unimpressive appearance, he enjoyed a high reputation. He participated often in *renga* and in *wakan*, a kind of *renga* which had links in both Chinese and

Japanese. Yūko, thanks to his Buddhist training, often supplied the Chinese verses in a *wakan*, as in 1591, when he joined with Jōha and Hosokawa Yūsai. He studied poetics under the masters of the day, Yūsai and Kujō Tanemichi. His *waka* are in the conventional Nijō style without much individuality, but he knew the traditions of the *waka* thoroughly. On one occasion, when Hideyoshi attended a formal poetry gathering, he kept Yūko close to him, and the poems he recited as his own were actually composed by Yūko. For all his great learning, Yūko was also not above writing comic poetry in the manner of Sōchō. He was abreast of all the latest literary fashions and helped to create them.

Perhaps his most lasting literary monument were the five Nō plays he wrote by order of Hideyoshi, who was extremely fond of Nō and did not hesitate to appear in even the most difficult roles, including *Sekidera Komachi*. That was, no doubt, the reason he asked Yūko to write some Nō plays which would glorify him and his accomplishments. The plays Zeami wrote for Yoshimitsu's court never touched on recent events, but were set in the distant past, as if to preserve the remoteness and grandeur of a world far removed from that of daily experience. But the plays written by Yūko in 1594 dealt with events still fresh in the minds of the audience. There is a connection between Yūko's historical accounts and his plays; *Shibata Taiji Ki* (The Subjugation of Shibata), written in 1582, was the source of the Nō play *Shibata* written eleven years later.

The *waki*-Nō *Yoshino-mōde* describes the visit of Hideyoshi to Yoshino in February of 1594. He was accompanied by Hidetsugi, Ieyasu, Jōha, Yūko, and others. According to the account in *Hoan Taikōki*, "Hideyoshi-kō had on his usual false whiskers, wore false eyebrows, and had his teeth blackened. The persons accompanying him were all dressed with the utmost beauty and created so splendid a sight that a crowd assembled to watch them." Once the party arrived at Yoshino, there was a large poetry gathering. The play *Yoshino-mōde* was apparently first presented on this very occasion. It opens with the *waki*, a courtier in the service of the present emperor, declaring, "The *taikō* and *daishōkoku* rules the country as he sees fit. He has pacified the three Han [kingdoms of Korea], and on top of this has acceded to the entreaties [for peace] from China. Having accomplished these brave deeds, he has returned and built a great palace in the village of Fushimi in the province of Yamashiro. And now, this spring he is making a pilgrimage to Yoshino to admire the cherry blossoms. I go to serve him."

The woman-play *Kōya-mōde* continues the story of *Yoshino-mōde*. Hideyoshi and his party have traveled from Yoshino to Mount Kōya where he has made offerings to the spirit of his mother. The *shite* in the first part of this Nō is an old nun, but in the second part she reappears splendidly attired as Hideyoshi's mother, who has gained the exalted status of Bodhisattva of song and dance thanks to the filial actions of her son! *Kōya-mōde* was performed during Hideyoshi's visit. The writing is skillful, the construction expert, and the language poetic. When Hideyoshi returned to Osaka he asked the Nō master Komparu Hachirō to choreograph a final dance for this play and he himself performed it.

Perhaps the most interesting of Yūko's Nō plays is *Akechi-uchi*. The *shite* is Hideyoshi himself, and the *waki* is not a priest or a courtier but Akechi Mitsuhide, the murderer of Oda Nobunaga. The play ends with Hideyoshi pursuing and killing Mitsuhide. This unconventional ending—the *shite* of a Nō play normally does not kill the *waki*—was a contribution to the evolution of Japanese drama.

Yūko's Nō plays were not performed in later times, and his histories have been neglected. Although he was one of the outstanding literary figures of the Sengoku period, when a new regime took over, his writings fell into disfavor. He was fortunate, however, that he died in 1596, two years before his master, and was thus spared the shame of having to recant.

It is easy to feel sorry for Yūko, who spent most of his life as a kind of court jester to Hideyoshi, but his own attitude was probably revealed in the sobriquet he chose for himself, Sōchūsai (Shrimp in the Seaweeds Studio), derived from the poem in the *Kokinshū*:

ama no karu	Like the *warekara*,
mo ni sumu mushi no	The shrimp that lives in
warekara[1] to	the seaweed,
ne wo koso nakame	Fishermen gather,
yo wo ba uramiji	I weep for what I've
	brought on myself,
	But feel no hatred for
	the world.

All that Yūko did was *warekara*, and though he lifted his voice at times in grief, he did not hate the world.

NOTE

1. *Warekara* is the name of a small crustacean, but it is used here also with its more common meaning, "of oneself."

HOSOKAWA YŪSAI

1534–1610

Hosokawa Yūsai, the fourth son of Ashikaga Yoshiharu, was a daimyo in his own right and the father of a major daimyo who had a stipend of over 400,000 *koku*. Although his name is seldom mentioned among the notable figures of the Sengoku period, in his own day he enjoyed an extraordinary reputation, especially as a man of letters. His disciple Matsunaga Teitoku wrote, "This Yūsai *hōin* is no ordinary man. He has appeared in our degenerate times as a reincarnation of Lord Teika, perhaps in order that he might keep the secret traditions of the various arts from being broken." Teitoku was convinced that the secrets of poetry had been passed intact from Teika to Yūsai like water from one vessel to another, and he was struck especially by the fact that both Teika and Yūsai died on the same day, on August 20. Teitoku so revered the memory of his teacher Yūsai that he never failed to observe

71

the anniversary of his death, and in his will he commanded his descendants not to forget services for Yūsai, even if they forgot his own.

Teitoku recorded his observations of Yūsai mainly in *Taionki* (Record of Favors Received), a work which (as the title indicates) describes his indebtedness to his various teachers. Among his teachers he praised the *renga* master Satomura Jōha, Kujō Tanemichi (the great expert on *The Tale of Genji*), but above all Yūsai. No doubt it flattered the young man to associate freely with a daimyo, but he carefully distinguished Yūsai from the typical, uneducated daimyos of the Sengoku period. Teitoku's portrait of the "typical" daimyo was not very flattering. No sooner did such men rise in the world, he felt, than they became arrogant, furnished their houses with the utmost luxury, decorated their persons, and stamped about, their feet pointing outwards, their eyes flashing angrily, a hand thrust into the fold of their kimonos, and their chests thrown out. In their private life they indulged their taste for fleshly pleasures and amused themselves singing *kouta* or playing the samisen. They neglected their bows and horses, hated writing anything of a literary nature, but were proud of their knowledge and spurned the advice of others. They gave no charity to needy people living on their domains, were avaricious, merciless towards the farmers, never made friends with anyone inferior to them, and accepted the flattery of servile and superficial people. They spent their nights carousing and slept so late in the mornings that they never managed to dispose of their business. In Teitoku's estimation, Yūsai was completely different from the "typical" daimyo. He did not look down on ordinary people, and though he was superlatively gifted in all the arts, he never belittled anyone. He was, in short, a benevolent ruler without a single fault.

Among Yūsai's accomplishments none earned him more esteem in Teitoku's eyes than the fact that he was the transmittor of the *Kokin Denju*, secret commentaries on the meanings of the poetry in the *Kokinshū*. Some of these secret traditions are still of value in understanding the *Kokinshū*, but the most celebrated parts of the *Kokin Denju* were the *kirikami*, explanations of the "three trees" or the "three birds," and other mysteries. The *kirigami* are incredibly trivial, but, as Wilde said, anything becomes interesting if it is kept a secret. The ostensible reason for keeping the *Kokin Denju* a secret was to prevent unworthy vehicles from distorting the profound truths of this knowledge. This was also the reason why certain mysteries of Buddhism were transmitted esoterically. Even today many secrets still exist in connection with the techniques of performing various traditional arts which are known only to the head of a school and a few chosen disciples.

In the case of the *Kokin Denju* the transmission was so restricted that any man who was privileged to learn the secrets was distinguished from all other human beings and treated with reverence. Even an emperor on one occasion was not permitted to learn the *Kokin Denju* because he was still under thirty. Before Hosokawa Yūsai inducted Prince Tomohito (the younger brother of the Emperor Go-Yōzei) into the mysteries early in 1600, he first asked the authorization of Tokugawa Ieyasu. Later in the same year, just before the Battle of Sekigahara, Yūsai was besieged at Tanabe Castle by a large army. Bitter fighting continued, and it seemed as if the castle would surely fall. The Emperor Go-Yōzei, probably at the prompting of Prince Tomohito, sent two major counsellors to the castle with instructions that they receive the secrets of the *Kokin Denju* from Yūsai, lest he be killed in the siege and the secrets perish with him. When this imperial command was transmitted to the troops both inside and outside the castle, the fighting at once abated. The imperial envoys were admitted to the castle and led by Yūsai into the keep. There he lighted incense and took out the boxes containing the *Kokin Denju*. Next he hung on the wall pictures of the three gods and the five shrines.[1] He instructed the Major Councillor from Sanjō, Lord Saneeda, in the mysteries and, as "a sign that the secrets of the Land of the Gods had been transmitted," he composed this poem:[2]

inishie mo	Words preserve
ima mo kawaranu	Seeds of the heart
yo no naka ni	Unchanged in this world,
kokoro no tane wo	Both in ancient times
nokosu koto no ha	And in the present.

The two major councillors subsequently sent word to Ishida Mitsunari, the attacking general, that since Yūsai had transmitted the *Kokin Denju* to the emperor, he was therefore the emperor's teacher. Mitsunari was asked to lift the siege at once; if he did not, he would be considered an enemy of the court. Faced with this threat, Mitsunari lifted the siege. Both friends and enemies of Hosokawa Yūsai believed that the preservation and transmission of the secrets of the *Kokin Denju* were more important than victory in a siege. I wonder if another such instance of the pen being mightier than the sword is to be found in history.

Of course, a knowledge of the *Kokin Denju* was not Yūsai's only claim to Teitoku's adulation. Teitoku described him as a master of the arts of both peace and war. Yūsai was peerless in the *waka*, *renga*, Nō, calligraphy, football, archery, horsemanship, and cookery. His conduct was always exemplary. Teitoku disapprovingly quoted an "unprincipled person" who claimed that Yūsai was weak as a soldier. Emura Senzai (1565–1644), the author of *Rōjin Zatsuwa* (Idle Gossip of an Old Man), also cast doubts on Yūsai's performance on the battlefield. He wrote, "He never achieved any distinction in battle. It is true that he was praised by Hideyoshi for having pitched camp successfully during the fighting in the province of Kai, but this was the only such instance." Teitoku argued that the reason why some people doubted Yūsai's martial abilities was that his elder brother was as "fierce as a wild boar"; in comparison to such a warrior Yūsai seemed unmilitary, but in fact "he had all kinds of exploits to his name." Teitoku supported his argument by citing an example of

Yūsai's prodigious strength: he was able to grasp an ox by the horns and force it to give way.

But above all it was as a literary man that Teitoku worshiped Yūsai. If we read Yūsai's criticism today, it is rarely of much interest. For the most part he was content to display his grasp of poetic lore in response to specific questions about the composition of *waka*. The following passage is typical:

"Question: Is it all right to mention the word 'flowers' in a poem in which one has already mentioned the patrinia blossoms?
"Answer: Yes, it is quite all right."

In all matters he looked to Fujiwara Teika for guidance: "The *Hundred Poems by a Hundred Poets* is a work which should be constantly consulted. It was for the sake of future generations that Teika vouchsafed to compile this work." Yūsai's own theories of the *waka* were extremely conventional. He stated as his conviction, "It is advisable to devote one's attention to the moon and the blossoms. In addition, one should give consideration to transience when writing poetry. It is quite unnecessary to search extensively for other aspects of importance." His collection of *waka*, *Shūmyō Shū* (Collection of the Wonders of Nature), was published by his great-grandson in 1671. It consists of over six hundred *waka*, none of them memorable. Yūsai's *renga* was of more interest. Although he often expressed contempt for *renga*, certainly when compared with *waka*, he in fact composed a good deal of *haikai no renga* (comic *renga*). One *hokku*, composed at the house of Ōmura Yūko in Osaka at a time when Hideyoshi was planning an invasion of China, was particularly brilliant. Seeing *karatachi* (trifoliate orange) blooming in the garden, Yūsai composed this verse:

karatachi wa	The *karatachi*
yagate sono mama	Before long, just as it is,
kikoku kana	Will be a *kikoku*.

The point of this verse is that *karatachi* and *kikoku* are two names for the same flower; but *karatachi* also means "departure for China" and *kikoku* also means "return to his country." Yūsai gained such fame for puns of this kind that, according to Teitoku, "even kids playing with dogs knew his *hokku*."

Yūsai displayed his wit on other occasions in such a way as to ingratiate himself with his superiors. One day Oda Nobunaga asked Yūsai in what year he was born. "In the same year as Your Excellency," he replied. (Nobunaga and Yūsai were both born in 1534.) "Then, you were born in the year of the horse?" "Yes, sir, but it was a different horse." "What do you mean, a different horse?" "Your Excellency's horse carries a saddle trimmed in gold, but mine is just a miserable packhorse always burdened with a load of debts." Teitoku, who reported this incident, commented, "Everybody present smiled with amusement."

On another occasion, when Yūsai composed *renga* with Hideyoshi and Jōha, Hideyoshi wrote this *hokku*:

okuyama ni   Deep in the mountains,
momiji fumiwake   As I tramp through maple
naku hotaru   leaves,
                             A firefly sings.

Yūsai at once added a *wakiku*, but somebody in the gathering murmured that fireflies do not sing. Jōha agreed with this criticism, much to Hideyoshi's annoyance, but Yūsai insisted that there was textual authority for saying that fireflies sang, and he quoted an ancient poem that ended, "Apart from the fireflies, no insect is singing." Hideyoshi's good humor was restored, and he praised Yūsai's deep understanding of *renga*. Some days later, when Jōha went to visit him, Yūsai expressed his surprise that a master of *renga* like Jōha should have exhibited such a lack of understanding of people's feelings. He admitted that he himself had made up the "ancient poem" on the spot in order to ease the tense situation. Here was a rare occasion when Jōha, who always chose the path of discretion, was given some pointers by an even greater master!

Yūsai is of special interest because of his exceptional artistic versatility. He was not only an accomplished poet and scholar of poetry but an outstanding musician, as we know from the testimony of a master drummer who declared that Yūsai's performance on the instrument was so brilliant he would never forget it as long as he lived. Yūsai was at once a preserver of the old culture, exemplified by the *Kokin Denju*, and a contributor to the new. His salon provided poets like Matsunaga Teitoku with the opportunity for creating the artistic *haikai no renga*.

Yūsai leaves the impression of having been a particularly easygoing daimyo, but he had another side. Modern critics have praised the "open-minded attitude" he displayed in transmitting the *Kokin Denju* not only to members of the court but to generals like Shimazu Yoshiyuki (1533–1611). But he never granted his disciple Teitoku this privilege. Teitoku wrote, "On the twenty-fourth of November, 1593, I went with my father to call on Hosokawa Yūsai. He took us to the back room of his house, where he opened a box and showed us the contents, saying, 'These are all the secret books of the tradition. Look at them!' There were four books of different sizes with the words 'transmitted texts' on the covers." That was as close as Teitoku ever came to being instructed in the *Kokin Denju*. For all his "open-minded attitude," Yūsai was a daimyo, and he must have considered that a great difference separated him from even a well-born young man like Teitoku. He was in any case highly aware of his own importance, an attitude that was especially apparent during the siege at Tanabe Castle. According to some accounts, he at first rejected the efforts of the emperor to save his life, saying that it was his duty as a soldier to die fighting. But it did not take long to persuade him that he and the traditions he preserved were worth more than a victory, or even a soldier's honor.

NOTES

1. There are at least three different lists of the "three gods" (*sanjin*). Perhaps the most appropriate three are those associated with poetry: the gods (*myōjin*) Sumiyoshi and Tamatsushima and the *Manyōshū* poet Kakinomoto no Hitomaro. The "five shrines" (*gosha*) also are identified variously, but the most common use seems to be as a designation for the Inari Shrine at Fushimi, south of Kyoto.

2. Other sources state that the poem was composed earlier that year, when Prince Tomohito received induction into the mysteries of the *Kokin Denju*.

KINOSHITA CHŌSHŌSHI

1569–1649

Any man who lived in the Sengoku period was certain to be faced with disagreeable and difficult choices. The writers who survived this period unscathed either had an instinctive ability to guess which side would win in a dispute, or else had the agility to desert a loser instantly, as soon as they realized they had backed the wrong man. But the changes were so rapid and so intense that even the most adroit operator sometimes made serious mistakes. How, for example, could the *renga* master Jōha have guessed that the *kampaku* Hidetsugi would one day be punished as Hideyoshi's most deadly enemy? Among those who made no major mistakes in their friendships were some who, though experiencing moments of grief because of their decision, considered it necessary to turn on their relatives in order to save their own skins. Hoso-kawa Yūsai's daughter was married to a son of Akechi Mitsuhide, but when Mitsuhide assassinated Nobunaga and it became clear that Mitsuhide and Hideyoshi would soon fight to the death for supremacy, Yūsai unhesitantly cast his lot with Hideyoshi. Nevertheless, it must have been painful to abandon members of his own family. Probably that was why he shaved his head and became a Buddhist monk on the very day that Mitsuhide killed Nobunaga. Later in his career, after the death of Hideyoshi, Yūsai again had to make a difficult decision, whether to continue his allegiance to Hideyoshi's family or to shift to Tokugawa Ieyasu, the rising power. He chose Ieyasu. That was why Ishida Mitsunari, an ally of Hideyoshi's, besieged Yūsai at Tanabe Castle. After the siege was lifted, he retired to Kameyama, a castle near Kyoto originally built by Mitsuhide. In 1603 the Shogun Ieyasu appointed Yūsai as his court antiquarian. This time Yūsai went to live in a hermitage at the foot of Kinugasa Mountain in Kyoto, where he planned to spend his remaining years. Yūsai successfully served Nobunaga, Hideyoshi, and Ieyasu, but in an age of shifting loyalties, nobody even criticized his inconstancy!

Soon after Yūsai died in 1610, his disciple Kinoshita Chōshōshi wrote a short but moving eulogy. Since Chōshōshi did not actually attend his teacher's funeral, which was held at Kokura Castle, where Yūsai's son Tadaoki was now the lord of the castle, he could not describe the magnificent ceremonies that honored Yūsai. But his grief over the death of his teacher is unmistakable, despite the archaic language in which this short account is phrased. It is not clear exactly what Chōshōshi studied under Yūsai, but no doubt he learned, in the medieval tradition, the secrets of poetry. Perhaps Yūsai also initiated Chōshōshi into a study of the *Manyōshū*, the foundation of the *waka* in the Kinsei period. But Chōshōshi's poetry would be known for its freshness and unconventionality, rather than for its fidelity to the orthodox traditions espoused by Yūsai.

Perhaps Chōshōshi originally began his study of poetry under Yūsai merely as a polite diversion suitable for a soldier. He came from a minor samurai family which rose to a position of great importance thanks to two fortunate marriages. His aunt became Hideyoshi's wife, and his daughter married Tokugawa Ieyasu's fifth son. The aunt's marriage brought the entire family material advantages. Chōshōshi was given court rank and allowed to use the surname Hashiba, then Hideyoshi's surname. (Later, when Hideyoshi adopted the surname Toyotomi, Chōshōshi also called himself by that name.) In 1587, when he was only seventeen years old, Chōshōshi was appointed lord of Tatsuno Castle, and, in 1592, when the Korean expedition was organized, Chōshōshi followed Hideyoshi to Nagoya in Hizen. In 1594 he was appointed an acting general and was named lord of the castle of Obama in Wakasa, a post that carried an income of 81,500 *koku*.

The death of Hideyoshi in 1598 cast a pall over Chōshōshi's career, but he continued to serve the Toyotomi family. Two years later the relations between the Toyotomi and Tokugawa families worsened until finally warfare broke out. Chōshōshi's father, Iesada, was enfeoffed in Himeji Castle and took the side of the Tokugawa. The choice was apparently more difficult for Chōshōshi. He was under conflicting orders from Toyotomi Hideyori and Ieyasu to defend Fushimi Castle. Among the defenders of the castle against an attack by Ishida Mitsunari was Torii Mototada, a passionately devoted follower of the Tokugawa, who managed, with a handful of supporters, to hold off a vastly superior encircling force until he died fighting. Now Chōshōshi was faced with a terrible decision. Should he, like Mototada, defend the castle to the death against the forces of Mitsunari, or should he remain faithful to his old connection with the Toyotomi family? This was the kind of situation in which Japanese warriors traditionally committed *seppuku*, but Chōshōshi instead fled the castle and went into retirement in Kyoto. In the meantime, troops from his castle at Obama had been engaged during his absence in the siege of Tanabe Castle where Yūsai, his teacher, was trapped. The strange coincidences of warfare afflicted Chōshōshi at every turn.

After the Battle of Sekigahara later in 1600, Chōshōshi's lands were taken from him by Ieyasu, and his behavior, which was considered a violation of the samurai code, subsequently came under attack from many quarters.

The *waka* poet Ozawa Roan (1723–1801), for example, declared, "He was temperamentally unsuited to being a soldier. It was ignoble of him when, under siege at Fushimi, he panicked at the situation and left Torii Mototada and the others to die." Even Chōshōshi's admirers had difficulty in justifying Chōshōshi's unmartial conduct. One anonymous biographer wrote, "When Fushimi Castle was under siege, the Lesser General of Wakasa [Chōshōshi], a certain Torii, and various others were in the castle. Torii was a retainer of Lord Ieyasu, and that is why he died fighting at this time. The Lesser General left the castle. People at the time spread word that this was because he was lacking in martial courage, but more thoughtful people said that if he had sided with Mitsunari at the time he would have been unfaithful to Lord Ieyasu, but if he had remained in the castle he would have gone counter to the way of his ancestral obligations. Accordingly, his decision to abandon the world and live in the mountains neither violated his ancestral obligations nor betrayed his friend. Similar examples must surely exist in China, and the Lesser General acted as he did because he had learned the teachings of the sages."

I confess that I am more impressed by Chōshōshi's painful decision to flee the castle than I would have been if he had committed *seppuku* in the usual manner. To die would have been easy for a samurai, but to live and face men's reproaches must have been difficult. Perhaps Chōshōshi was emboldened to take this step by his realization that another life, as a poet, was open to him.

His poetic talent was already apparent in such early compositions as the account of his journey to Kyushu, in which he already displayed his characteristic style, elegant but simple, written almost entirely in *kana*. The text is poetic throughout. Indeed, it is rather surprising, considering that this journal was kept by a young samurai on his way to conquer China (as he supposed), that he was moved less by the thought of the glories awaiting him on the battlefield than by the places mentioned in poetry and other famous sights he passed on the way. The elegiac tone of his writing suggests some medieval wandering priest rather than a man of a new era of continental conquest. In the diary, moreover, Chōshōshi recorded *waka*, and even a *chōka* composed on the way, and he quoted the *Manyōshū*. Unlike most of the warriors, who died fighting during the Sengoku period, Chōshōshi obviously had his mind set on poetry rather than on power or glory.

Chōshōshi described in his essay *Sanka no ki* (An Account of my House in the Mountains) the little house in which he lived in genteel poverty after he had decided to give up his life as a samurai. The house was in the Higashiyama district of Kyoto. He wrote, "I have had tile roofs put over the two ten-foot-square rooms where I normally spend my time. On the wall in-between the rooms I have hung cardboard squares (*shikishi*) on which I have copied poetry by Tu Fu and especially moving *waka* by the poets of old. I have also written beside them my own clumsy poems, composed when my feelings were too strong to let them pass unrecorded. Since no one else is likely to see these poems, I am sure I will be forgiven the sin of immodesty. In this way I pass half a day at a time. If a visitor comes and robs me of my peace and quiet, it might seem as if I had been deprived of my solitariness, but how could the conversation with a close friend be without value?" Many years later Bashō in his *Saga Diary* would quote the last lines, an indication of how completely he associated himself with Chōshōshi's feelings.

Elsewhere in *Sanka no ki* Chōshōshi wrote about his library, which he called *Dokushō* (Solitary Laughter). It contained 1,500 *kan* (scrolls) of Chinese books, and about 260 volumes of Japanese books, including poetry matches, romances, and collections of old *waka*. This was a first-class library for that time, and he lent books even to such Confucian scholars as Fujiwara Seika (1561–1619).

Chōshōshi, unlike most poets of his day, never attempted to turn his gifts to financial profit. Poetry was his avocation, his chosen way of passing the years free of military or political duties. He once told an intimate, "I know nothing about the art of poetry. I merely express, for my own amusement, what I have thought in my heart." Chōshōshi undoubtedly exaggerated his dilettantism; certainly he was a serious student of the poetry of the past, especially by Shōtetsu, whose unconventional themes appealed to him more than the lifeless Nijō school poetry he had learned from Yūsai. Chōshōshi, though he undoubtedly knew most of the "secrets" treasured by teachers of the *waka*, never sought paying pupils, nor even spiritual disciples. He maintained an air of detachment from the concerns of such professional poets as Matsunaga Teitoku, but Teitoku and his friends attacked him, apparently because certain rich disciples had deserted Teitoku to study with Chōshōshi. Teitoku's adherents pointed out the failings in Chōshōshi's poetry, by which they meant the departures from orthodox rules. Chōshōshi replied by accusing Teitoku of allowing his poetry to be defiled by the dust of the world. Teitoku's writings, he declared, were "close to vulgarity and not poetry. He conducts himself like a beggar."

It was not possible for Teitoku to lead Chōshōshi's kind of unworldly life. He had no choice but to sell his talents in order to make a living. This certainly makes him seem less attractive to us than Chōshōshi, but Teitoku was the forerunner of the professional writers of the future, whereas Chōshōshi belonged to the more elegant world of the past where poetry was engaged in as a gentlemanly pursuit. He is often treated as a transitional figure, between the Sengoku and Kinsei periods, but even though most of his life was spent under the Tokugawa regime, it is rare to find in his poetry a reflection of the new age. It should not be forgotten, however, that it was his fortunate connection by marriage with the Tokugawa family which saved him from severe punishment after he abandoned Fushimi Castle, and which enabled him to live like a gentleman afterwards.

Chōshōshi's poetry enjoyed unusual popularity in its day. Children sang his poems and townsmen inscribed them on fans. People responded especially to his style, much freer and more imaginative than that of other *waka* poets of the time. But even though this non-professionalism was appealing, it did not necessarily make for poetic excellence. Rather than search for poetic genius or even marked individuality in the *waka* by Chōshōshi, it is best to savor quietly a poem like:

kado sashite	The house I live in
yaemugura seri	Has its door bolted by weeds;
wa ga yado wa	It's east of the capital,
miyako no higashi	At the foot of Eagle
washi no yamamoto	Mountain.

This poem even has a touch of realism in its mention of where Chōshōshi actually lived, though it was a familiar convention for poets to write of their houses being overgrown by weeds. Other poems suggest direct observation:

matsukaze wa	The wind blowing
fukishizumarite	Through the pines has calmed
takaki e ni	And on the high branches
mata nakikawasu	Again the spring thrushes
haru no uguisu	Are calling to each other.

Occasionally we catch an unmistakably personal tone:

yoyo no hito no	When I realize
tsuki ni nagameshi	The moon is the memento
katami zo to	Of the brooding

> omoeba omoeba   Of generations of men,
> mono zo kanashiki   How sad everything seems!

Such *waka* attracted many poets to Chōshōshi, but he was viciously attacked by the court poets for his indifference to their standards of good taste.

Chōshōshi lived to be eighty. He read his books, wrote poetry when so moved, associated with such friends as Yūsai, Seika, and Kobori Enshū (1579–1647). The quiet elegance of his life appealed to people of his day. It is no less appealing today, though it would be hard to imitate him. His manner of life was close to that of the Chinese *bunjin*, or the Japanese gentleman described by Yoshida no Kenkō in *Tsurezuregusa* (Essays in Idleness). Some years before his death he composed his farewell poem for the portrait now at the Kōdai-ji:

> tsuyu no mi no   Even though my dew-like
> kiete mo kienu   frame
> okidokoro   Will disappear, there will be
> kusaba no hoka ni   Another place where
> mata mo arikeri   It will rest, unvanishing,
>   Away from the grass and the
>   leaves.

It is a touching poem, and it suggests that he was aware that the life he led had been a beautiful one, in spite of the agonizing decision he had to make at Fushimi Castle, and that many men of the future would envy him.

MATSUNAGA TEITOKU

1571–1653

Matsunaga Teitoku is usually described as a poet of the Tokugawa period, but his formative years were spent during the Sengoku period, and the men to whom he was most closely bound
were Sengoku figures—his teachers Satomura Jōha and Hosokawa Yūsai, Ōmura Yūko who wanted to adopt Teitoku as his
heir, and Kinoshita Chōshōshi, even though he was his greatest
enemy.

Teitoku was born in the age of Oda Nobunaga. As a young
man he served as a scribe to Toyotomi Hideyoshi and studied
classical literature with impoverished nobles of the imperial court.
He knew Christian converts, had one brother who was exiled and
another who traded with the Portuguese and died in the South
Seas. His own life was full of paradoxes. Though a conservative
in his outlook on life and taste in poetry, he became the acclaimed

leader of the newest movement in poetry; though he bitterly regretted that his relatively humble birth did not permit him to
share fully in the court traditions, in the end he devoted himself
to the education of classes lower than his own. He became the first
important figure of Kinsei literature.

Teitoku was the second son of Matsunaga Eishu, a professional
renga poet. His paternal grandfather, the daimyo of Takatsuki,
could trace his family back to the late Heian period, when his ancestors fought on the side of Minamoto Yoritomo. His paternal
grandmother claimed descent from Fujiwara Teika. But in 1541,
when Eishu was only three, his father was killed in battle, and two
years later his mother died. The boy, deprived of family support,
was sent to the Tōfuku-ji, a center of Zen studies in Kyoto. Eishu
was later converted to Nichiren Buddhism, and his children were
brought up in this faith. Eishu returned to the laity before he was
twenty, and soon was making a living as a teacher and corrector
of poetry. His excellent education and family connections enabled
him to associate familiarly even with the Daimyo Hosokawa Yūsai. Thanks to his father's acquaintances, Teitoku received instruction even as a child from the best scholars.

Teitoku wrote relatively little about his father in his autobiography *Taionki*. One passage relating to his father, however,
stands out. In 1573, when Teitoku was two years old, fighting
broke out in Kyoto between supporters of Nobunaga and those of
Ashikaga Yoshiaki (1537–97). The inhabitants of the city fled,
seeking refuge in the countryside. Eishu, his wife, and their four
children headed north. Teitoku wrote, "The worst point was
when we came to a mountain torrent where waves boiled furious-
ly over the rocks. Wading across was out of the question, and
there was only a narrow log bridge. My father, taking one small
child under his right arm, and leading my sister (who was only
five) with his left hand, slowly moved sideways over the log. My
mother stood on the near shore, one baby on her back and the
other in her arms, watching him. I remember her telling me how,

when my father reached the middle of the bridge, his face looked paler than the waters below."

This early experience may explain Teitoku's conspicuously timid and conservative disposition. Though he was proud of his samurai ancestry, he recalled with horror the warfare he had witnessed as a child, and rejoiced in the peace and stability of the Tokugawa regime. He declared that the debt he owed the shoguns was "higher than the mountains and deeper than the sea." It is easy for us today to assume that this praise was sycophantic, in the manner of Ōmura Yūko praising Hideyoshi, but for someone who had lived through the chaos of the Sengoku period, the blessings of peace must have been deeply appreciated.

When Teitoku was six, he and one of his brothers, who was two years older than he, both expressed the wish to become Buddhist priests. Eishu, unwilling for both sons to become priests, asked them to draw lots. The elder brother won and soon afterwards entered a Nichiren sect monastery where he studied under Nichiō, the celebrated exponent of the extremist doctrine of *fuju fuse* "receive nothing, give nothing."[1] This brother accompanied Nichiō into exile and died on Tsushima. Teitoku remained a devout believer throughout his life. But for an accident in the drawing of lots, he might never have written any poetry.

Eishu recognized Teitoku's precocious gifts and sent him to study *waka* with the courtier Kujō Tanemichi (1507–94), revered as a repository of the authentic poetic traditions. Tanemichi must have been impressed by the boy. Not only did he instruct him in *waka*, but he transmitted to the eleven-year-old boy the secret traditions of *The Tale of Genji*, which consisted of how to pronounce the names of emperors or the *nengō*. It is unbelievable that Tanemichi should have entrusted a child, no matter how brilliant, with such secrets, but a manuscript survives of the *renga* in one hundred links, composed in 1582 to celebrate Teitoku's induction into the mysteries. It begins:

hana ni nao   Still shall I offer

michiwake soen yukue kana	Guidance among the blossoms; The path lies beyond. *Kujō Tanemichi*
haru wa kasumi ni hikarenuru sode	In the spring how one's sleeves Are tugged ahead by the mists. *Matsunaga Teitoku*
taka tobō susono no kigisu nakisutete	The hawk soars above Mountain fields where the pheasant Leaves its song behind. *Hosokawa Yūsai*

These verses are by no means memorable, but they convey the teacher's delight in his student, the pupil's gratitude for the guidance he has received, and the distinguished guest's admiration not only for the boy (the hawk) but for the boy's father (the pheasant). Ōmura Yūko also took part in this *renga* sequence.

By the standards of the time Teitoku was fortunate to have studied under Tanemichi, but what he learned would be of little interest today. The mind boggles at the thought of the boy spending months memorizing the secret traditions. Yet Teitoku, at least until late in life, never questioned that this was what scholarship meant. Nor had he any doubts about the lifeless poetry of the Nijō school in which Tanemichi guided him. But Teitoku was aware that he could never be recognized as a master of the *waka*, regardless of his skill, because he was ineligible to be initiated into the mysteries of the *Kokin Denju*.

It may have been for this reason also that Teitoku's father sent the boy to study *renga* with Satomura Jōha, despite the bad relations that prevailed between Jōha and himself. Jōha gladly accepted the boy as his pupil because of his talent, even though he could not pay the usual fees.

Tanemichi disapproved of Teitoku's studying *renga*. When

Teitoku asked him the best way to improve his *waka*, he replied, "The first thing you should do is give up *renga*." For him *renga* was a new and vulgar form of poetry, and he feared Teitoku would pick up bad habits. Teitoku did not follow his advice, but undoubtedly he took greatest pride in his *waka*. His *waka* are monotonous and boring, but Teitoku was convinced that a good *waka* neither depended on originality of conception, nor on the expression of deep feelings, but on the exact compliance with the rules of poetic composition laid down by the founders of Japanese poetics. The restriction imposed on his range of expression by these rules did not frustrate Teitoku. He had no burning emotions that demanded voice in his *waka*.

In 1603 Teitoku made friends with an important man twelve years his junior, Hayashi Razan. Razan decided to offer public lectures on the interpretation of the Confucian texts he had been studying, and he asked Teitoku to lecture on *Tsurezuregusa* (Essays in Idleness). Teitoku was reluctant to take the unprecedented step of lecturing publicly on traditions he had learned privately, but he finally consented. As so often in his life, Teitoku's initial reaction, the product of his naturally cautious and conservative attitudes, was shaken by other people's enthusiasm. Teitoku delivered lectures "to the crowd" on *Essays in Idleness* and *Hyakunin Isshu* (A Hundred Poems by a Hundred Poets). Both works, though they were to be of enormous importance in the education of all classes during the Tokugawa period, had up to this time been relatively obscure. Teitoku's lectures marked the end of the medieval tradition of secrecy in the study of classical texts.

The nobles' reactions to Teitoku's lectures were predictable. Nakanoin Michikatsu, his teacher of *Essays in Idleness*, was furious. Teitoku, far from resenting his criticism, felt deeply ashamed of himself, but the course of his future activities as a bringer of "enlightenment" had been set. In later years he founded a school for children of the samurai class in Kyoto and wrote textbooks for use in teaching.

Teitoku seems to have earned a comfortable living between his teaching and his guidance of aspiring poets. He considered that his primary vocation was writing and correcting *waka*, but for years he had also been composing *renga*, both serious and comic. In time he came to be esteemed as the outstanding poet of *haikai no renga*. Teitoku was not proud of this reputation and treated his own compositions with little respect. *Haikai* poetry, he believed, was no more than impromptu witticism, unworthy of being recorded. When his disciples asked permission to publish a collection of his *hokku* and *tsukeku*, Teitoku refused, saying that the word *shū* (collection) could not be used for so lowly a form of poetry. Even after this collection, called *Enoko Shū* (Puppy Collection), had appeared, Teitoku refused to associate himself with it. The postface spoke merely of a "certain old gentleman" who had looked over the manuscript. But the collection attracted such favorable attention that Teitoku reconsidered his negative stand. Despite his wishes, he had been enthroned as the chief figure in the world of *haikai*.

Teitoku's *haikai* in no way compare to the superb creations of Bashō or Buson. We sense nothing like a world reduced to a microcosm, or the poet's experiences presented in their most evocative essentials. Such ideals were foreign to Teitoku. Even when he grudgingly came to admit that writing *haikai* could be more than a game, he never supposed that it could be the vehicle for man's deepest emotions. His efforts were concentrated on purifying *haikai* of vulgar elements and establishing standards of excellence. His only justification for writing *haikai* was in rather negative terms: in the Latter Days of the Buddhist law people could no longer write *waka* with the grandeur displayed by the old masters; *haikai* poetry was therefore better suited to a degenerate age.

Teitoku's *haikai*, unlike his *waka*, acquired depth with time; though their interest lay primarily in the increasing awareness they displayed of the legitimacy of such poetry. He originally dismissed *haikai* as a mere diversion. He moved then to tolerating it as a poetic form written in a lighter mood than *renga*. Finally, under pressure from his disciples, he defended *haikai* as a verse form with distinct aims of its own.

Teitoku's greatest contribution to Japanese literature was to elevate the *haikai* to a position of dignity worthy of a serious man's consideration. Most men of his day had supposed that *haikai*, unlike *waka* or *renga*, was a mere "spewing forth of whatever came to one's lips." Teitoku, though at first he agreed with this opinion, gradually came to recognize that *haikai* had legitimate functions, at the very least, this familiar kind of poetry could interest men in more elevated varieties. The *haikai* he wrote towards the end of his long career go beyond his usual plays on words and various forms of pedantic humor, but even this poetry is not of much interest today. He failed as a poet, but if he had not established the composition of *haikai* as a legitimate occupation and provided it with its basic rules, Bashō and the other masters might not have chosen this form of poetry. *Haikai* might have remained the kind of entertainment at which Sōchō or Yamazaki Sōkan excelled after a session of serious *renga* had been completed, or the brief flashes of wit in which Hosokawa Yūsai delighted. Teitoku turned *haikai* into a demanding and respectable art. His place in literary history is assured, as the reluctant innovator who transformed the traditions of the Sengoku period into the formative elements of the new Kinsei poetry.

NOTE

1. According to this doctrine, it was wrong for believers in Nichiren Buddhism to conduct transactions with non-believers.

THE KINSEI PERIOD (1600–1867)

The years between 1600 and 1867 are known by various names to Japanese scholars. Often they call it the Tokugawa period, after the name of the family which in 1603 established the shogunate. They also call it (especially in works treating literature of the time) the Edo period, because the city of Edo (modern Tokyo) was the seat of the Tokugawa shogunate. But it is perhaps most commonly known as the Kinsei period, *kinsei* meaning "recent generations."

The Tokugawa shoguns from the beginning of their regime were obsessed with the need for order. This sentiment can probably be explained in terms of the chaos that prevailed through most of the fifteenth and sixteenth centuries. Elaborate precautions were adopted to keep local military figures from ever aspiring to overthrow the government, and Confucianism was adopted as the state philosophy, no doubt because of its insistence on the importance of a stable, well-run government. Finally, in order to keep foreign countries from threatening Japan, the country was closed to almost all other countries. Nagasaki, where there was a Dutch trading station and a Chinese colony, was the only city which retained some of the cosmopolitanism of Japan in the late sixteenth century.

This closure of the country was initially beneficial to Japanese literature. The establishment of peace and security enabled people to devote more time to literature and the arts. Moreover, the lack of foreign influences promoted the growth of indigenous elements in artistic expression. The *haiku* poetry of Bashō, the novels describing contemporary life by Saikaku, and the *jōruri* by Chikamatsu made the end of the seventeenth century a particularly brilliant period of Japanese literature. These men also had imitators, rivals, and disciples, some of considerable distinction.

Although the regime was organized as a military state, there was virtually no warfare for well over two hundred years. Members of the samurai class, which had the responsibility for defending the shogunate, had no occasion to use their arms, so they turned to literature and other cultural pursuits to gain distinction. They wrote not only for their own class but for the *chōnin*, the townsmen, who made up the populations of the great cities of Kyoto, Osaka, and Edo. Only in the early nineteenth century would literature written by the *chōnin* themselves come to be of major importance.

Towards the end of the period there were attempts made by the government to restore the integrity of the samurai class. The Kansei Reforms of 1787 to 1793, and the Tempō Reforms of 1841 to 1843, were in the end unsuccessful in stemming the tide of dissatisfaction with the regime.

At the close of the Kinsei period members of the samurai class openly or covertly expressed disaffection with the regime. Many called for a return of power to the emperor. Some believed that the country should be opened to commerce with the rest of the world, others that the foreigners who had been allowed to reside in Japan ever since Commodore Perry "opened" the country in 1853 should all be expelled. With the exception of Kabuki drama, the late Kinsei period was a bad time for literature, no doubt because the prevailing uncertainties did not provide a congenial atmosphere for writers.

TAKARAI KIKAKU

1661–1707

In Japan the traditional relationship between master and disciple is so deeply rooted that it has not disappeared even today, when so much of the pre-modern culture has been rejected. To become the disciple of a celebrated master has been considered not only an honor, but often as a step absolutely essential to the economic as well as the spiritual well-being of a young man. In the distant past there were extreme examples in China and Japan of the determination shown by young men who desired to be accepted as disciples of the great masters. Hui-kuo demonstrated the strength of his resolve to become Bodhidharma's disciple by cutting off his left arm. Ikkyū was so convinced that only Kasō Sōdon could give him the instruction he craved that he endured repeated humiliations in order to be guided by his chosen master.

The need for suitable disciples was no less essential to the masters. Kūkai (Kōbō Daishi; 744–835) related how, when he arrived in China, he was joyfully welcomed by the master Hui-kuo, who declared, "I knew that you would come! I have been waiting for such a long time. What pleasure it gives me to look on you today at last! My life is drawing to an end, and until you came there was no one to whom I could transmit the teachings." Although Hui-kuo had many Chinese disciples, he had not found one capable of bearing the full weight of the esoteric Buddhist teachings. Instinctively, from his first glimpse of the Japanese priest, he recognized that at last he had found his true disciple, the man who would continue his teachings. Kūkai also described how, after Hui-kuo's death soon after he had transmitted his learning to Kūkai, Hui-kuo appeared to him in a dream. He urged Kūkai to pass on the esoteric teachings to Japan, and predicted that if in his next reincarnation he was born in Japan, this time he would be Kūkai's disciple.

It is not surprising that few of the great literary figures of the past were blessed with disciples capable of continuing their work. The lightning that strikes a genius at birth cannot be summoned at will from the skies, nor will prayer or diligence compensate for a lack of the touch of lightning. Saikaku, for example, had disciples, but their names are remembered today only by specialists in the literature of the Kinsei period. This does not mean that he lacked influence; on the contrary, Saikaku's influence was so great that for a whole century no writer of fiction escaped it. But he seems not to have inspired the special, lasting relationship that prevailed between other Japanese masters and disciples.

The writer of the Kinsei period who attracted the most disciples was undoubtedly Bashō. This was partly because writing *haikai no renga* was a communal literary art that required companions, but no other *haikai* teacher had so many followers. At the time of Bashō's death, there were more than two thousand disciples scattered all over the country, and the number of self-styled disciples kept growing. Anyone who had ever joined in composing *haikai no renga* with a disciple of Bashō's proudly claimed to be a disciple himself. This naturally annoyed the "direct disciples," who probably numbered no more than sixty, and one threatened to denounce the impostors. But Mukai Kyorai (1651–1704), one of Bashō's most important disciples, cautioned him: "The Master was so generous that he usually raised no objection when people styled themselves his disciples, making no distinction among them, whether they were noble or humble, close to him or hardly known. . . . If the people you mention say that they belong to the school of our master Bashō, you should let it go at that." Kyorai also once stated why he thought so many men claimed to be disciples of Bashō: "Some look up to him because of the character he reveals in his poetry, for his qualities of serenity and sincerity, and are delighted to join with him in making *haikai*. Others are attracted by his reputation of being a great poet and follow him out of respect."

Bashō gladly accepted these disciples. For one thing, he needed their financial support, but above all, as a true teacher, he was anxious to ensure that his style, the *Shōfū*, not perish with him. One can infer his feelings from an example of more recent times: the poet Masaoka Shiki was heartbroken when Takahama Kyoshi (1874–1959) refused to become his successor, fearing that his art of *haiku* would die with him. The desire to have disciples is little different from the desire to have children and see oneself reflected in one's progeny.

Bashō was proud of his disciples. In 1680, when he himself had not yet established his reputation as a poet, he published a collection of *kasen* (*haikai no renga* in thirty-six verses) by twenty disciples. In the years that followed Bashō showed himself to be at once dependent on his disciples and their main source of strength. Near the end of his life, when he was painfully ill, he journeyed all the way to Nagoya to patch up a quarrel that had arisen among some disciples. Even his earlier travels were largely occasioned by his desire to see old disciples and to make new ones. He was re-

markably fortunate in his relations with his disciples, though at
the end of his life he seems to have realized that he, like any artist,
must travel alone:

kono michi ya	Along this road
yuku hito nashi ni	There are no travelers—
aki no kure	Nightfall in autumn.

Among all the disciples Takarai Kikaku occupied a special place.
He was probably Bashō's first disciple after he had decided to
accept pupils and establish a "school" of *haikai* poetry in Edo
about 1677. For almost twenty years the two men were on the
closest terms as master and disciple, but Kikaku, for all his love and
admiration of his master, led a completely different life. He was a
typical Edo man of the time—a hard drinker and a frequenter of
the licensed quarters (though one critic averred that Kikaku was
physically excited only by fish!). He has accordingly had the reputation of being a frivolous poet, a sycophantic clown who considered composing *haikai* to be merely a pastime. This reputation
is certainly unfair to Kikaku, but its long persistence indicates how
differently he was considered from his master.

Kikaku was the son of a physician and was himself trained in
this profession. He received an excellent education in the Chinese
classics, paintings, and calligraphy. From the time he first became
a pupil of Bashō's, at about the age of sixteen, he showed exceptional skill at incorporating his Chinese learning in *haikai* composition, though his quick wit and readiness with an allusion
sometimes served mainly to mask a rather shallow mind. A certain disciple once asked Bashō what he had been able to teach a
man so unlike himself as Kikaku. Basho replied: "My style favors
solitude and is delicate; Kikaku's favors flashiness and is delicate.
The delicacy marks him as belonging to my school." Bashō was
genuinely fond of Kikaku, despite their dissimilarities, as we can
infer from a famous passage in *Kyorai-shō*:

"kiraretaru   Stabbed in a dream—
yume wa makoto ka   Or was it reality?
nomi no ato   The marks of a flea.

Kyorai said: 'Kikaku is really a clever writer. Who else could
have described so completely so trifling an experience as having
been bitten by a flea?'

The Master said, 'Yes, he is a Lord Teika. The same sort of thing
might be said of him as of Teika, that he went on writing about
things of no great importance as if they were extremely profound.' "

No doubt there was irony in Bashō's comment, but he did not
lightly compare his disciples to Teika.

Kikaku's unwillingness (or inability) to follow his master's style
illustrates another aspect of the relationship between master and
disciple. The disciple chooses a particular master because of the
special respect he feels for him and seeks to model his work on his
master's. However, he usually also experiences a contrary impulse
to display qualities that are peculiarly his own and not those he
admired in his mentor. The personal relationship between the two
men may remain intimate, but the intellectual or artistic antithesis
is apt to grow. Indeed, unless there is some antithesis, the disciple
will never develop his individuality and become a master himself.

Kikaku's *haikai* were much admired, and he was usually placed
at the head of the ten outstanding disciples of Bashō. His rival
disciple Morikawa Kyoriku once wrote, "If any verses in the different collections attract attention, they generally prove to be by
Kikaku. I don't know of any other disciple in his class." Kyorai
replied, "If I were to rate him in terms of the magnitude of his
talents, I would have to place him above my head, but if I rated
him on the baseness of his verses, I would set him beneath my
feet."

Kyorai's remark indicated disapproval not only of Kikaku's
personal life, but of the themes of his poetry, which seemed to

have been chosen as if to emphasize the differences between Bashō and himself. One feature of his poetry which may have irritated fellow disciples was its unusual obscurity. Kikaku's collection *Minashiguri* (Empty Chestnuts), compiled in 1683, included this *haikai*:

ka wo yaku ya	Burn the mosquitoes—
Hōji ga neya no	In Pao-ssu's bedchamber
sasamegoto	Lovers' whisperings.

In order to understand this verse we must recognize the allusion to the story of Pao-ssu, the grim-faced consort of King Yu of the Chou Dynasty. When all other attempts to make her laugh had failed, the king, in desperation, lit the beacon fires used to summon his feudal lords, even though he was not in danger. The plan worked: Pao-ssu was moved to laughter by the sight of the feudal lords galloping up only to discover there was nobody to fight. Unfortunately, however, the king was overthrown when the feudal lords failed to respond to his next lighting of the beacon fires, this time in earnest. In Kikaku's verse "burning" suggests the lighted stick used to burn mosquitoes that have intruded into the mosquito netting, and recalls the beacon fires lighted to summon the feudal lords. Mention of Pao-ssu's name evokes a romantic scene of lovers whispering together inside a mosquito netting.

Bashō sometimes mentioned Chinese people and events in his *haikai*, but never for so frivolous a reason, and the erotic atmosphere is not found either. But Kikaku's assertion of his own distinctive manner did not displease Bashō; in his postscript to *Minashiguri* he likened Kikaku's poetry to the works of Li Po, Tu Fu, Saigyō, and Po Chü-i—high praise indeed. Kikaku's poetry has undoubtedly become much more difficult to understand today than it was for readers of the Genroku period, who instantly recognized most literary allusions. Perhaps Kikaku's greatest achievement as a poet was his success in stimulating an interest in *haikai* among the intellectuals of Edo, including the Confucian scholars, who no doubt welcomed references to Pao-ssu and similar historical figures. But even if, after reading an extensive commentary, we can admire Kikaku's skill at condensing several layers of meaning into one short poem, his works rarely move us in the way that Bashō's masterpieces do. This is apparent especially when the two men wrote on similar themes.

In 1692 Bashō composed the *hokku*:

shiodai no	The salted bream
haguki mo samushi	Look cold, even to their
uo no tana	gums,
	On the fishmonger's shelf.

Perhaps his interest in this everyday scene was stimulated by Kikaku, who often described ordinary events, but how different is the verse on a similar theme composed by Kikaku two years later:

koe karete	Their voices are hoarse,
saru no ha shiroshi	And how white the
mine no tsuki	monkey's teeth!
	Moon over the peak.

Kikaku, characteristically, alluded to a theme of Chinese literature, monkeys dolefully crying in a gorge. It is a night in late autumn and, as the monkeys cry, the moonlight catches the white flash of their teeth. The whiteness of the teeth, an element not found in Chinese poetry, gives this *hokku* its peculiar quality. But there is something unpleasantly contrived about the image. It contrasts with Bashō's unaffected perception of a cold-looking fish, microcosm of the bleakness of the city in winter. Kikaku was so proud of his verse that in his collection *Kukyōdai* (Elder and Younger Brother Verses; 1694) he matched it against Bashō's and judged it was the "elder brother." It is true, though, that he also praised Bashō's verse for having attained the realm of *yūgen*. Bashō recognized a certain similarity as well. He once remarked that it

was the "unaffected" quality of the last line that marked this as a poem in his style.

Kikaku's verse on the monkeys managed to pack a cluster of desolate images into the seventeen syllables: the hoarse voices of the monkeys, the chilly white of their teeth, the cold, distant moon; and beyond what he stated in the poem there was the background in Chinese literature apparent in the choice of a typical Chinese theme. But Bashō's verse achieved an even more powerful effect because it stemmed from a single, uncontrived perception. Kikaku refused to adopt the style of *karumi*, or simplicity, that Bashō advocated in his last period, perhaps because he was aware that his special talent consisted in the display of the very kind of ingenuity which Bashō had rejected. He must also have recognized that a verse in the *karumi* style not inspired by Bashō's genius risked being nothing more than a flat statement.

He seems deliberately to have chosen subjects that Bashō would have avoided. Some poems are not difficult to follow and have the lilt of a children's song or a folk song.

At times he also displayed greater personal feelings in his poetry than Bashō ever allowed himself, as when he described his youngest daughter lying in her coffin, or his emotions on digging his father's grave. He also wrote on such contemporary subjects as the celebrated vendetta of the forty-seven retainers of the Lord of Akō, a subject which moved him especially because three of his own disciples were among the retainers. There is even an occasional note of social criticism in his poetry, a quality not easily found in Bashō's. Indeed, his poems are so remote from the typical manner of Bashō that it may surprise us that he was considered a loyal disciple to the end. When in 1691 *Sarumino* (The Monkey's Raincoat), the outstanding collection of *renku*, was compiled, Kikaku was asked to write the preface.

Kikaku, by a strange twist of fate, was present at Bashō's deathbed. He had gone to Osaka without even knowing his master was ill, but a premonition took him to his master's side. Once he arrived, the other disciples all deferred to Kikaku, recognizing the special bond between the master and his first disciple. Kikaku's account of Bashō's death was his last tribute to his master. The two men were entirely dissimilar, but their bonds were deep and unbreakable.

KI NO KAION

1663–1742

Genius is a rare commodity in any age. Even if one does not restrict the word "genius" to Leonardo da Vinci, Shakespeare, Mozart, and the few other men whose achievements surpass that which can reasonably be expected of human beings, extremely few men in each century are likely to be remembered five hundred years later. Yet, paradoxically, geniuses and near-geniuses have tended to appear in clusters rather than one at a time. This phenomenon was described thirty years ago by the American anthropologist A.L. Kroeber in his massive work *Configurations of Cultural Growth*. He noted, for example, that the three greatest playwrights of the French theater, Corneille, Racine and Molière, were contemporaries and their period of activity lasted less than forty years. The next important cluster of French playwrights, those of the Romantic period two hundred years later, were also contemporaries. The same kind of clustering holds true of the Greek, the English, and the German theaters. And, of course, it is true of Japan too. The great playwrights of Nō, Kannami, Zeami and Zenchiku, wrote most of the standard plays of the Nō repertory in a relatively brief period. The next flowering of the Japanese theater did not occur for three hundred years, when a few dramatists, notably Chikamatsu Monzaemon and Ki no Kaion, wrote the plays which, in revised forms, have become the staples of both *jōruri* and Kabuki theaters.

Kroeber stated that he saw "no evidence of any true law in the phenomena dealt with; nothing cyclical, regularly repetitive or necessary." He made no attempt to explain why geniuses have tended to appear in clusters, but instead described instances from every civilization and in every branch of the arts and sciences. He noted also that although clusterings of geniuses are usually national, they sometimes have crossed boundaries, as we know from various simultaneous but independent discoveries and inventions, such as the devising of calculus (by Newton and Leibnitz), the discovery of oxygen, the invention of the telephone. The same holds true of such aesthetic innovations as the first use of a metrical form, a musical chord, or a technique in painting. He might also have mentioned the creation of the *sewamono*—the tragedy of the common man, as opposed to the tragedies of kings and generals—which began with Chikamatsu's *Sonezaki Shinjū* (Love Suicides at Sonezaki) in Japan and was followed less than thirty years later, quite independently, by similar works in Europe.

The student of Japanese culture will immediately think of many clusters of geniuses. For example, Izumi Shikibu, Sei Shōnagon, and Murasaki Shikibu were all writing at about the same time, but never again would there be a similar group of such extraordinary women writers. The *waka* has been composed for over a thousand years, but only during relatively brief periods has a cluster of geniuses produced poetry of the highest quality. A cluster of great poets created the anthology *Shin Kokinshū* in 1205, but for centuries afterwards hardly any *waka* of value were composed.

The phenomenon was recognized two thousand years ago by the Roman historian Velleius Paterculus, who attributed the clustering of geniuses in different fields of human endeavor to the emulation of one genius by other men, whether out of envy or admiration. Other writers have explained this phenomenon in historical terms, using such expression as "the time was ripe" for some discovery or artistic progress. For example, the victory of the English over the Spanish Armada has been cited as the source of the energy that produced the great period of the English drama, and the securing of national peace after the Battle of Sekigahara (1600) has been cited as the source of Genroku culture. Perhaps there is truth in such historial reasoning but, as Kroeber pointed out, these explanations are more often wrong than right, because they provide only one element of a large complex of historical causes. Periods of peace and prosperity do not necessarily coincide with those of great cultural achievements. Almost all the great Roman writers were dead by the time that Augustus gave peace to the realm, and the next important surge of literary activity took place under the worst of the Roman emperors, including Caligula and Nero.

I have no new theory to advance as to why, for example, Japanese literature flourished so brilliantly in the Genroku period. Certainly it was not because the Shogun Tsunayoshi encouraged fiction, puppet plays, or *haikai* poetry. He had only scorn for such plebeian forms of literature, and he certainly did not approve of the *ukiyoe*, the characteristic pictorial art of the time. Perhaps the historian should avoid attempting to explain why a sudden cluster of geniuses like the novelist Saikaku, Bashō, and Chikamatsu simultaneously appeared. Nevertheless, I wonder if Velleius was not on the right track when he spoke of emulation as a cause for the sudden emergence of clusters of men working in the same artistic field. Sometimes there was direct imitation or even plagiarism, as in the case of Saikaku's followers, who shamelessly borrowed whole passages from his works. But sometimes also, as in the case of Ki no Kaion, we can sense a real desire to emulate.

Chikamatsu Monzaemon, indisputably a man of genius, appeared on the scene as if from nowhere, creating works of great literary value for a theater which had previously depended on crude or moralistic texts written by men who were ashamed to sign their names to the works. His *Love Suicides at Sonezaki* not only created a new form of *jōruri*, the *sewamono*, but enjoyed enormous popularity. The Takemoto Theater, which had been in financial straits, prospered, and the chanter Takemoto Gidayū became so famous that the name *gidayū* is now a common noun designating a variety of singing. It is not surprising that an ambitious man should have attempted to lure some of Gidayū's customers to a new theater. The man was Toyotake Wakadayū, a pupil of Gidayū's who was so faithful to his master that he was reputed even to imitate Gidayū's manner of sneezing. He founded the Toyotake Theater in 1703 as a rival theater, and the first work he presented was a crude adaptation of *Love Suicides at Sonezaki*, challenging the success of the Takemoto Theater.

Various difficulties compelled Wakadayū to close his theater in the following year, but he reestablished it in 1706, this time inducing Tatsumatsu Hachirobei, the leading puppet operator of the day, to join him. For his staff playwright he chose Ki no Kaion.

Kaion, the son of an Osaka townsman, spent almost all his life in Osaka. His family ran a long-established cake shop which purveyed to the imperial court, and the household was extremely cultured. Kaion's father was an amateur poet who had studied under Matsunaga Teitoku, and his elder brother was the celebrated *kyōka* poet Yuensai Teiryū. Kaion received an excellent education, but his first choice of profession was not that of a literary man but of a Zen priest. A short biography written years after his death stated that dissipation caused Kaion to give up the priesthood. Perhaps this same dissipation enabled him to write so familiarly of the pleasure quarters, in the accustomed manner of a *jōruri* dramatist.

It is not clear when Kaion wrote his first play. Two works performed at the Toyotake Theater during its first unsuccessful season in 1703 have been attributed to him, including the imitation of *Love Suicides at Sonezaki*, and they show some resemblances of style to his later works. Perhaps he wrote these plays as a mere diversion, testing his powers as an amateur in writing for the theater. Although these two plays do not impress a modern reader, Wakadayū must have detected in them the makings of a genuine dramatist, and his confidence was rewarded when in 1708 Kaion wrote his first important *jōruri, Wankyū Sue no Matsuyama.* This story of Wanya Kyūemon, a rich Osaka merchant, and his love for Matsuyama, a courtesan from the Shimmachi pleasure quarter, was based on events that had occurred about twenty-five years earlier. It was by no means the first play to have been derived from this source, and Kaion borrowed much from his predecessors. He succeeded, however, in giving the material a much more dramatic structure than any previous work had shown, and the play is surprisingly plausible and moving. If we compare it to Chikamatsu's later play based on a similar theme, *The Uprooted Pine* (1718), it is apparent that it lacks Chikamatsu's stylistic brilliance, but it is more economically handled, with no unnecessary scenes or characters inserted for the sake of variety or in order to evoke the stirring sensations of *ninjō* (human feelings). It has frequently been observed that Kaion tended to emphasize *giri* (duty) at the expense of *ninjō*. It is true that *Wankyū Sue no Matsuyama* has no scenes like the game of *shōgi* between Yojibei's father, Jōkan, and his father-in-law, Jibuemon, in which Jōkan reveals that, despite his apparent miserliness and reluctance to part with his money to save his son's life, he truly loves the son, or the later passage in which Jōkan, under pretense of describing a mouse in a trap, is actually urging his son to escape from household confinement. Such scenes were undoubtedly effective with an audience which had come to the theater to enjoy the intoxicating beauty of Chikamatsu's language and the histrionics of the chanters, but they seem contrived and even unnecessary when read today. One wishes at such places that Chikamatsu had exerted Kaion's control over *ninjō*.

Giri can be a cold and unpleasant quality, especially when it compels people to perform acts of formal compliance to society which they oppose in their hearts, but an excess of *ninjō* can be detrimental as well. Chikamatsu himself once stated, "There are some who, thinking that pathos is essential to a *jōruri*, make frequent use of such expressions as 'it was touching' in their writing, or who, when chanting, do so in voices thick with tears. This is foreign to my style. I take pathos to be entirely a matter of restrain. It is moving when the whole of a play is controlled by the dramatic situation, and the stronger and firmer the melody and words, the sadder will be the impression created. For this reason, when one says of something which is sad that it is sad, one loses the implications, and in the end, even the impression of sadness is slight."

The head of Bunshichi, a common Bunraku character

Chikamatsu, unfortunately, did not always live up to this dictum. In many scenes the expression of the emotions is embarrassingly detailed. Kaion, on the other hand, seems deliberately to have avoided such displays of emotion, and as a result he sometimes achieves a power of expression that surpasses even Chikamatsu. Kaion's best play was probably *Yaoya Oshichi* (Oshichi, the Greengrocer's Daughter), written about 1715. The story was made famous by Saikaku's version in *Five Women who Loved Love*, where it is given a light-hearted, almost comic treatment. Oshichi and her family are evacuated to a temple because a fire broke out in their neighborhood. At the temple she falls in love with the young priest Kichiza, but she is forced to leave him when the family returns after the fire has been extinguished. In her rather simple-minded way she imagines that she will be able to see Kichiza again if there is another fire, so she starts the fire which eventually burns down most of Edo. Although at the end she is punished by being burnt at the stake, we feel little sympathy for her, no doubt because Saikaku's treatment has kept us at such a distance from the character that she never develops into a full human being.

Ki no Kaion started with the same basic facts, but he used them to create a tragedy. In his play Oshichi is transformed from an impetuous tomboy into a woman who gives way to her emotions under the strain of unbearable pressure. Her father, we learn, borrowed two hundred *ryō* to rebuild his house after the first fire. Buhei, who lent the money, suddenly demands either the return of his money or Oshichi in marriage. The mother urges Oshichi to marry Buhei, promising to help her to obtain a divorce immediately afterwards. Kichiza, who overhears part of this conversation, decides he would be in the way of Oshichi's happiness, and he leaves without seeing her. Oshichi is frantic when she discovers that Kichiza is gone, and in her distraught state of mind she conceives of setting a fire as the only way to avoid a hateful marriage and rejoin her lover.

The greatest difference between Kaion's play and Saikaku's novel occurs in the third act. Saikaku mentions, but so briefly that one almost misses the point, that Oshichi's body turned to melancholy smoke. But Kaion's play evokes the full horror of a burning at the stake. Oshichi's parents are shown as blaming themselves for having driven her to commit such a serious crime by insisting on a repugnant marriage, and express disillusion that all their devout prayers over the years to Buddha and the Japanese gods have been in vain.

While the parents reproach themselves, preparations go ahead for the execution. The parents anxiously pray for rain to extinguish the pyre, but on that fateful day the morning sun shines brightly. There follows a *michiyuki*, not a lovers' journey as was usual in Chikamatsu's plays, but Oshichi being paraded from the prison to the execution grounds. The passage is a moving blend of reminiscences and present emotions: "Let anyone who wishes to call me human scum, let anyone laugh who wishes. My love was the first I ever knew, and it has been undivided. Even if my body is transfixed, my bones ground to powder, my flesh turned to ashes, my soul will remain in this world and follow his shadow, clinging to his body. Hand in hand with my husband, for two lifetimes or three, we will in the end mount the same lotus blossom."

No sooner does Oshichi reach the execution grounds than Kichiza pushes his way through the crowd. He is dressed in white, a sign he is resolved to die. As he begs the guards to execute him with Oshichi, she says, "How foolish you are, dear Kichiza. I have nothing in the least to regret. My crime was of my own choosing. Now that I have seen you, I desire nothing else before I die. Your life is precious. Please become a priest and pray for me, pray hard for me when I am gone." The officials refuse to kill Kichiza, but in despair, crying out that life is meaningless now, he plunges a dagger into himself.

No one reading this play, which is one of the masterpieces of the Japanese theater, could accuse Kaion of lacking *ninjō*. It is incredible that this excellent play is no longer performed. Kaion, using virtually the identical materials which Saikaku fashioned into an amusing tale, was able to create a true tragedy. The tremendous though foolish gesture of Oshichi lifts her above the ranks of conventionally unhappy young women and makes her a creature of passion who gladly risks the most terrible consequences to be with the man she loves.

Kaion has also been accused of having insufficient poetic imagination. It is true that his texts seem prosaic when compared to the finest sections of Chikamatsu's masterpieces, but when compared to the *jōruri* written during the next fifty years, including such famous plays as *Chushingura*, his language is not only poetic but embued with stylistic distinction. The audiences at the Toyotake Theater appreciated especially the verbal play of which Kaion was a master.

Ki no Kaion has often been dismissed as an imitator of Chikamatsu, but unlike the later dramatists who wrote the revised versions of Chikamatsu's plays that are now performed, adding impossible twists of plot in order to surprise the audiences, Kaion's versions do not seem to imitate but rather to challenge Chikamatsu's use of the same materials. The critics have uniformly preferred Chikamatsu's *The Courier for Hell* to Kaion's *Keisei Sandogasa*, not only because of the lyrical beauty of Chikamatsu's play but because the impetuosity shown by his hero Chūbei is more appealing than the calm determination of Kaion's Chūbei, who is aware almost from the beginning of the play that he is traveling on the road to death. I too prefer Chikamatsu's play, but Kaion's *Keisei Sandogasa* definitely is a work of importance.

The influence did not go only in one direction. Not only did Chikamatsu's *The Uprooted Pine* show Kaion's influence, but his last *sewamono*, *Shinjū Yoi Kōshin*, was performed sixteen days after Kaion's *Shinjū Futatsu Haraobi* on the same theme, and in this case (at least in my opinion) Kaion's play is superior.

In his own day Kaion enjoyed almost as great fame as Chikamatsu. "He ranks alongside Chikamatsu," wrote one critic. An account of the rivalry between the Takemoto Theater and the Toyotake Theater indicates how greatly the two theaters stimulated each other. The fact that another genius was writing at the same time seems to have inspired Chikamatsu and enabled him to create dramas that gave him his eminence as the greatest dramatic poet of Japan.

It might have been expected that with the death of Chikamatsu in 1724 Kaion would have become the undisputed master dramatist of *jōruri*, but although he lived on until 1742, his last play was written before Chikamatsu's death. We do not know why Kaion failed to write any plays during the last twenty years of his life, but perhaps the death of Chikamatsu deprived Kaion of a master to emulate, using Velleius' words. Perhaps he felt, like the celebrated Kabuki actor Nakamura Kichiemon after the death of his great rival Onoe Kikugorō, that being a genius is intolerably lonely when one is deprived of a cluster of peers.

A Bunraku narrator's lectern

KAN CHAZAN

1747–1827

For most educated men of the Kinsei period Chinese was not a foreign language. Boys of the samurai class especially learned Chinese by rote, at first not understanding what the words meant. In later life they used it as the special language of their class. If they wrote poetry, it was generally *kanshi* (poetry in Chinese), whether they were describing their heroic sentiments in the face of death or their pleasure in the company of a beautiful woman at an inn overlooking a river. In spite of the fact that they were writing *kanshi*, very few were interested in learning the pronunciations given to the characters by the Chinese themselves. They associated the writing of *kanshi* and *kambun* (prose in Chinese) with China only to the extent that they felt obliged to allude to Chinese landscapes and people in their compositions. For a samurai of the period who wrote his letters in *sōrōbun*, his essays in classical

Japanese, and spoke colloquial Japanese, Chinese seemed the appropriate medium for elevated thought in prose or poetry because he believed it possessed capabilities of expression not shared by a humbler variety of languages. That was no doubt why Kada no Azumamaro, when he addressed a petition to the shogun asking for a tract of land in Kyoto where he might promote the study of the Japanese classics, wrote it in classical Chinese rather than the language of the ancient Shinto prayers.

In the more distant past Chinese had been used to record the history of Japan, and a knowledge of Chinese poetry was essential to a courtier of the Nara or Heian period because his ability at composing *kanshi* sometimes determined his chances of promotion. As early as 751 the *Kaifūsō*, a collection of *kanshi* written by members of the court, was compiled, perhaps in order to demonstrate to visiting Chinese that the Japanese were genuinely cultured. In the Heian period Sugawara no Michizane (845–903), esteemed today as a god of learning, was known especially for his *kanshi*. Although Michizane's *kanshi* are still of interest today, the *kanshi* written by most other Japanese of the Heian period or later are conspicuously unoriginal by modern standards. Phrases and even whole poetic conceptions were freely borrowed from poems of the past. Indeed, a *kanshi* which was completely original and failed to echo masterpieces of the past was considered to be faulty. For Japanese, moreover, it was doubtless reassuring to quote from some Chinese master when writing what was, after all, not their native tongue, though we know from the examples of such men as Kūkai or Michizane that it was possible for some Japanese to write flawless and even elegant Chinese.

In the Kamakura and Muromachi periods the chief practitioners of Chinese learning were Buddhist priests. They wrote poetry not only of religious but entirely secular content, assuming the roles of Chinese gentlemen admiring picturesque landscapes and enjoying the pleasures of this world. The *kanshi* by Ikkyū, though not highly praised by experts on *kanshi*, are especially affecting for modern readers precisely because he chose to ignore the old models and write directly from his heart.

The question arises as to why Japanese for so many centuries wrote classical Chinese, a language totally unlike the one they normally spoke. If composing *kanshi* and *kambun* had been nothing more than exercises in which they demonstrated their mastery of a foreign language, their writings would surely be as completely forgotten today as the answers to last year's entrance examinations in English for Tokyo University. Obviously something more elevated was involved. The Japanese clearly felt that certain sentiments could be more adequately expressed in Chinese than in Japanese. It is difficult, however, to define precisely what these sentiments were. A person reading *The Tale of Genji* or *The Tale of the Heike* is not likely to feel that the Japanese language was incapable of expressing subtle or deeply moving emotions. Indeed, the language of such Heian masterpieces as *The Tale of Genji* or *The Tale of Nezame* is extraordinarily effective in expressing the nuances of the internal lives of the characters. Not only is there nothing in Chinese fiction superior to these works, but the Chinese language does not seem to lend itself so readily to such refinements of expression.

The peculiar appeal of Chinese for educated Japanese is intelligible in terms of the parallel experience in Europe. During the Middle Ages Latin was the language of the church (as classical Chinese was of Buddhism and Confucianism). It was an international language, and scholars from all over Europe worshipped and attended lectures delivered in Latin together. Scholars from within the orbit of Chinese civilization with its multitude of languages and dialects could similarly "speak" to one another with their brushes. Even after Latin had ceased to be a truly international language, as the result of the religious upheavals in Europe, it remained the language of learning and refinement. In the poem *Philip Sparrow* by John Skelton (c. 1460–1529) a young woman explains why she prefers to write Latin to English:

> Our natural tongue is rude,
> And hard to be ennewed
> With polished tones lusty;
> Our language is so rusty,
> So cankered, and so full
> Of frowards, and so dull,
> That if I would apply
> To write ornately,
> I wot not where to find
> Terms to serve my mind.

The English language, in other words, was considered to be too crude to express refinements of thought, and to be merely the language of daily life.

A century later Ben Jonson chided Shakespeare for knowing small Latin and less Greek. Today this fact is of no significance, and we are astonished instead by the incredibly rich vocabulary of English that Shakespeare used. Even in the 17th and 18th centuries, the period corresponding to Kinsei, many Englishmen continued to write poetry and prose in Latin, sometimes on formal occasions, sometimes also for expressing intensely personal feelings, as if Latin was closer to their hearts than English.

The Japanese *kanshi* poets of the Kinsei period seem to have found Chinese more congenial than Japanese. By borrowing words from the poems of some Chinese who lived a thousand years before they felt they could rise above the trivial joys and sorrows of daily life and link themselves with eternity. They took it for granted that men of their education would not write *waka* or *haikai* except in moments of levity, and that even then *kyōshi* (comic poems in Chinese) would be more to their tastes.

The *kanshi* written by the poets of the first half of the Tokugawa period have a bad reputation. They are derivative, uninspired, often badly expressed. But even the worst of these *kanshi* inevitably has more content than even the best *waka*. The five or seven syllables in a line of a *waka* have been likened to the five or seven characters in a line of a *kanshi*, but this comparison is inappropriate. A single word like *narinikeri* which is translatable as "was," can constitute a line of a *waka*, but a line of a *kanshi* usually consists of five or seven distinct words. For the poet who wished to suggest a scene or state of mind with the barest of means the Japanese form of poetry was perfect, but he could state a great deal more in a *kanshi* than in a *waka*.

Only in the second half of the Tokugawa period did the *kanshi* of the Kinsei period achieve maturity. The first really striking original poet was Rikunyo (1734–1801), a monk of the Tendai sect, who wrote such poems as the following:

Frosty Dawn
When I awoke on my dawn pillow, the frost was half evaporated,
And the clear sunshine, filling the window, was already warm.
From my bed I watched cold flies cluster on the other side of the panes,
Rub their legs together, fall, then fly up once again.

This description of a winter morning indicates actual observation. We are convinced that Rikunyo actually saw the flies through the translucent paper of the *shōji* as they weakly rubbed their legs, dropped to the floor, then flew up to the *shōji* again. Even if he borrowed phrases from some Chinese poet, the experience was his, and not the stereotyped evocation of a conventional scene.

The new style in *kanshi* was perfected by Kan Chazan. Unlike most earlier *kanshi* poets, Chazan was not a samurai, but came from a wealthy farming family which also brewed saké. As a young man he studied the Confucian classics and medicine in Kyoto and Osaka, but returned to his native town, Kannabe in Bingo Province, and founded a school there. Although Chazan was not a disciple of Rikunyo's, his *kanshi* were in Rikunyo's tradition, and his first collection had for a preface two letters he had received from Rikunyo. Both men were inspired by Sung poetry which was concerned with ordinary scenes of daily life and the emotions they called forth. The following poem, a perfect example of this new attitude toward *kanshi*, evokes a hot summer afternoon in Kannabe:

> More than twenty days without rain in this valley town;
> The river is beginning to dry in the shoals and shallows.
> At noon the whole town buzzes with locusts from
>   the pagoda-trees;
> A mountain boy, keeping close to the houses, sells sweetfish.

The images all contribute to the heavy atmosphere typical of a hot summer afternoon in Japan: the dinning of locusts, the drying of the river, the boy keeping under the shade of the eaves as he goes from house to house with his fish. The simplicity and sincerity of this poem is suggested by Chazan's lines, "I listen to children's songs and enjoy their simplicity; I am not ashamed to devise poems about them."

Chazan's poetry struck many people of his time not merely as unconventional but even outlandish. Hirose Tansō, later famed as a scholar and poet of *kanshi*, wrote that when, at the age of fourteen, he read a quatrain by Chazan including the verse, "I love to watch a great moon climb, embracing the pines," he thought the line was unorthodox, if not heretical. This was the poem that so startled the young Tansō:

> In the southern hall, waiting for someone, I do not light the
>   lamps;
> Insect cries from the four walls sound clear in the night air.
> Pointing at the peak ahead, I keep my guest sitting with me—
> I love to watch a great moon climb, embracing the pines

The image of the full moon "embracing the pines" must have bewildered most readers by its unusual use of personification.

However, when Tansō got to know Chazan's poetry better be began to appreciate it: "Chazan's poetry derives its style from Rikunyo's. The poems of Rikunyo are rich in descriptions, but convey few emotions, and they are excessively dense. Even if one can at first enjoy them, one is apt to dislike them later on. Chazan's poetry is half emotion and half description. He strikes a balance between thin and dense. That is why, as I discovered, one does not dislike it even after long acquaintance."

Even though Chazan spent most of his life in a remote part of the country, he knew most of the leading poets and artists of his day, thanks to his visits to Kyoto and Edo. He was friendly with the painters Ike no Taiga and Buson in Kyoto and Tani Bunchō in Edo. Among *waka* poets he knew well both of Kamo no Mabuchi's leading disciples, Katō Chikage and Murata Harumi. In an interesting passage in his essay *Fude no Susabi* (The Pleasures of the Brush), Chazan spoke of the art of the *waka* as *onnamoji*, "women's language," presumably because the *waka* was written mainly in *kana*. Ever since the Heian period *kana* writings had been associated with women, and writings in Chinese—considered of much greater dignity—with men. *Otokomoji*, "man's language," the counterpart of *onnamoji*, referred to poetry and prose in Chinese. He wrote of his two friends who were *waka* poets: "Kōkei and Harumi both compose skillfully in the man's language also. When Harumi met me he said, 'The men who wrote *waka* in the old days were for the most part Confucian scholars. You can tell that from the court ranks of the compilers of the *Kokinshū*." Obviously the *waka* poets were on the defensive when they talked with a master of *kanshi*, the man's language. Chazan apparently composed many *waka*, but only a few are preserved.

Among all his friendships none was more complex than that with Rai Sanyō (1780–1832). Chazan recognized Sanyō's unusual talents even when the latter was still a boy, and years later, when Sanyō was disinherited and in disgrace, Chazan invited him to be a teacher at his school, the Renjuku. Sanyō benefited greatly from

Chazan's kindness, and Chazan showed his admiration for the younger man by asking Sanyō's opinions of his *kanshi*. But the thirty-two years' difference in age and the totally dissimilar temperaments of the two men made clashes inevitable. Unlike Chazan, who enjoyed the quiet life in Kannabe, Sanyō was intensely bored by the lack of urban amenities. He was also disappointed with Chazan's school and wrote, "The pupils increase every day, but they are all apprentices, and there is not a genuine student among them. There is no satisfaction in teaching them."

Personal relations between the two men became so exacerbated that Chazan realized it was hopeless attempting to keep the brilliant Sanyō in the rustic milieu of Kannabe, and he arranged for him to go to Kyoto. An anecdote suggests the tense atmosphere before Sanyō left: "When Sanyō was about to leave for Kyoto, he wrote on the wall of the Renjuku, 'The mountains are ordinary, the water common, the teacher silly, and the students stupid.' It was always his habit while in the Renjuku to refer to Chazan as 'Bald Head,' so one day when he returned from outside, he asked a pupil, 'Is Bald Head inside?' Chazan, dressed in a formal kimono, respectfully opened the sliding door and said 'Kan Taichū is here.' Sanyō, taken aback to hear Chazan refer to himself by an extremely dignified title, bowed to the ground before he knew it and showed his respect."

Sanyō's later development as a *kanshi* poet outstripped Chazan's. His themes were more ambitious, his expression more intense. He became known for patriotic poetry, and especially for his devotion to the imperial family. But Chazan incorporated an ideal of the gentleman scholar that is not yet dead, and he inspires greater affection with his *kanshi* because they express in understated language a detachment from worldly concerns that permitted him to take pleasure in the smallest event and discover in it a pointer to the cosmos. This was surely the ideal of *otokomoji*.

TACHIBANA AKEMI

1812–1868

During the Kinsei period immense quantities of *waka* were composed all over the country. Most of this poetry is completely undistinguished, despite the care, scholarship, and intelligence demonstrated. In reading the *waka* of even the most accomplished Kinsei poets, we find ourselves looking not for any particular qualities of the poets themselves but for influences from the past or else for minuscule clues that reveal that the poems belong to this period rather than to some indeterminate or even distant past.

The most important group of *waka* poets of the seventeenth and eighteenth centuries were those who rediscovered the eighth-century collection *Manyōshū* and attempted not only to absorb its poetry but to revivify its ideals of simplicity and "masculinity." In most cases these poets were associated with *kokugaku* (National Learning), so called so as to distinguish it from Confucian or

Buddhist learning, both of foreign origin. Other poets, notably those at the imperial court, still revered the *Kokinshū*. But no matter how divergent the views on poetry that different men might have held, their expression tended to be remarkably similar. Cherry blossoms and maple leaves, spring mists and autumn rains provided the imagery for poets of every school. Some attempted to enrich their vocabulary by including forgotten words from the *Manyōshū*, but nobody followed the *haikai* poets in using colloquial language or words of Chinese origin. The result was that even a poem inspired by deeply felt emotions can hardly be distinguished from the most conventional expressions of grief over falling blossoms or deer separated from their mates.

The *kokugaku* scholar with the greatest literary talent was Kamo no Mabuchi (1692–1769). The *waka* he wrote before he was fifty were mainly in the style of the *Shin Kokinshū*. For the next fifteen years he composed poetry in the noble manner of the *Manyōshū*, perhaps in the hopes of persuading the Confucianists that Japanese poetry need not be restricted to descriptions of love or regret over the passing of time, typical themes of the *Shin Kokinshū*. His finest *waka* are in his *Manyōshū* style, notably a group of five composed in 1764 after moving to a new house.
Here is the first:

aki no yo no	The plains of heaven
hogara hogara to	Are bright and serene
ama no hara	This autumn night;
teru tsukikage ni	Through the shining
kari nakiwataru	moonlight
	The wild geese cross, crying.

This poem has been praised in the highest terms as an example of how Mabuchi had succeeded in making the *Manyōshū* tone a natural medium for his own expression. If it fails to impress us, this is not so much because the words and sentiments are faulty as because the content is so familiar. We may feel that Mabuchi is saying not what his heart compelled him to say but what the diction and mood of the *waka* permitted him to say. Was there nothing, we wonder, that a man living in the middle of the eighteenth century would have wished to express that was unknown a thousand years before? It is true that the experience of watching wild geese fly under the autumn moon was much the same as in the past, despite the great lapse of time, and a poet could be quite sincere in describing this experience in the old language, but we miss in this *waka* the individual voice of a particular poet.

The *waka* of the second half of the Kinsei period began after the death of Mabuchi in 1769, and its main characteristic was that the new poets were determined to express their own experiences in their own language. This does not mean that they resolutely turned their backs on the past. Even the most "revolutionary" of the new poets drew inspiration and often vocabulary from the *Manyōshū*, the *Kokinshū*, or the *Shin Kokinshū*. Nevertheless, the most interesting *waka* written after 1769 were not by the defenders of the precedents of the past but by men who advocated a new kind of *waka*.

The literary pronouncements of these poets are often stirring. The sharpness of their judgments, the vigor with which they denounced the dead weight of the past, and the urgency of their calls for a more vital kind of poetry make us turn eagerly to their *waka*, only to be disappointed. We expect poetry that will closely reflect the poet's emotions, be it anguish or ecstasy, his deep concern with the world he lives in, or at least some quirk of personality which distinguishes him from other *waka* poets, but the *waka* themselves at first glance seem almost indistinguishable from one another, and they closely resemble those of the rejected past. Even if the sentiments or the language surprise us by an unaccustomed earthiness or novelty of subject, the emotional impact of these *waka* is apt to be slight. A *waka* about a mouse is certainly an unusual departure from the normal range of subjects, but it may have little else to recommend it. Saigyō wrote about cherry blossoms as if their quickly fading petals symbolized the transcience of the whole world and man's deepest concern with the evanescence of life, but the Kinsei poets, whether they wrote of cherry blossoms or of mice, rarely suggest the distillation of a powerful experience.

Poets went on writing about the fragrance of plum blossoms not only because this was an established subject of the *waka* but because, like so many other elements in Japanese life, this aspect of nature and the importance attached to it had remained essentially unchanged. A city poet today could not without irony try to evoke the fragrance of plum blossoms in his poems because the chances of catching a whiff of this fragrance are rare in the age of industrial pollution. But in 1800, as in 800, the poet, even in the city, could enjoy the scent of plum blossoms announcing the arrival of spring, and it would recall to him, in the traditional manner, memories of friends of long ago. If poetic decorum forbade the poets of 1800 to describe what were actually the dramatic pleasures of their lives—sex, liquor, a good dinner, a promotion, or recognition of their work—it encouraged them to describe in much the same terms as their predecessors the secondary pleasures—the sights and sounds of the changing seasons, bittersweet reminiscences of love, the pleasure of travel to places with poetic associations. The Kinsei poets, as their predecessors, were convinced that the unchanging truths were the only important subjects of poetry and that, however new or unconventional the ways of describing them, there was basically no difference between themselves and the men who lived one thousand years earlier.

Readers today tend to prefer the poems that deviate most conspicuously from the conventions. The works of Ōkuma Kotomichi and Tachibana Akemi, both of whom died in 1868, the first year of Meiji, and who were the two most interesting *waka* poets of the late Kinsei period, suggest the limits to which the *waka* could be pushed without destroying it altogether.

Kotomichi was born in Fukuoka in 1798 into a family which had been distinguished for generations for its learning. As a young man, Kotomichi studied *waka* and later, under Hirose Tansō, also *kanshi*. He became so absorbed in his poetry that he neglected his family completely. His wife died young, apparently the victim of her husband's indifference to creature comforts. But not even this tragedy swerved Kotomichi from his study of *waka*.

Kotomichi was one of those poets who insisted on the contemporaneity of his *waka*. He wrote in a famous passage, "The masters of the past are my teachers, but they are not myself. I am a man of the Tempō era, not a man of old. If I were indiscriminately to ape the men of old, I might forget that I am a something-hachi or something-bei.[1] The surface meaning might then suggest the grandeur of a minister of state, and my poems would surely seem impressive, but they would be like merchants in noblemen's attire. It would be an act of pure imitation, like a performance of Kabuki."

Kotomichi's poems do not always live up to his prescriptions. He was by no means free of the conventional poetic diction, and his concerns were limited to elements of life he could observe in his house and garden. Political and social events of the time had little influence on him. But within their limitations, Kotomichi's poems have undeniable freshness of expression and conception.

A greater note of urgency can be found in the *waka* of Tachibana Akemi. He was born in 1812, and was the eldest son of a prosperous paper merchant in Fukui. The family believed it was descended from the eighth-century statesman Tachibana no Moroe, and Akemi claimed the surname Tachibana, a sign of his fascination with the Japanese past. As a young man he intended to become a Nichiren priest, but he changed his mind as he became more absorbed with poetry.

In 1833 Akemi went to Kyoto where he studied with a disciple of the loyalist *kanshi* poet Rai Sanyō for several months. Perhaps this contact was the source of the burning feelings of devotion to the imperial family found in his *waka*. He returned to Fukui and pursued the family business, but his heart was set on becoming a scholar and poet. In 1846, after the birth of his eldest son, he turned the business over to his half-brother and went to live in a retreat, where he gave himself to the study of the *Manyōshū* and the composition of his own *waka*. He lived in poverty, but his humble circumstances served as inspiration for some of his most affecting *waka*.

Akemi's first notable *waka* were written in 1860, after visiting a newly opened silver mine in Hida. Needless to say, the subject of these eleven *waka*, the silver mine, was hardly in the tradition of the *Kokinshū*, and they are a curious blend of realistic description and archaic diction.

hi no hikari	Inside a cavern
itaranu yama no	In the mountains where
hora no uchi ni	sunlight
hi tomoshiirite	Never penetrates,
kane horiidasu	Lighting lanterns they
	go in
	To dig out the precious
	metal.

The next *waka* is even more powerful:

mahadaka no	Stark naked,
onoko mureite	The men cluster together;
arakane no	Swinging great hammers,
marogari kudaku	They smash into fragments
tsuchi uchifurite	The lumps of unwrought metal.

Regardless of their intrinsic merits, these *waka* imparted a kind of strength to the medium it had never before possessed. Another new element in his *waka* was the political thought Akemi imparted to them. His patriotic convictions became apparent when in 1861 he worshiped at the imperial shrine at Ise and the imperial palace in Kyoto. His patriotism is also reflected in the following *waka* from his poetic sequence *Dokuraku-gin* (Solitary Pleasures):

tanoshimi wa	It is a delight
emishi yorokobu	In these days of delight
yo no naka ni	In all things foreign,
mikuni wasurenu	When I come across a man
hito wo miru toki	Who does not forget the divine land.

Other poetic sequences are even more conspicuously nationalistic, especially one called *Rendering Thanks to Our Country with Sincere Hearts*. The first *waka* of this sequence is:

masurao ga	A man of Yamato,
mikado omoi no	Thinking, in true sincerity,
mamegokoro	Of the imperial court,
me wo chi ni somete	His eyes bloodshot with staring,
yakiba misumasu	Readies his blade for action.

The *waka* does not lend itself readily to the expression of patriotic sentiments, and Akemi's righteous indignation seems constricted and somehow inadequate when cramped into thirty-one syllables. But since Akemi's materials were never used traditionally, one cannot doubt that these were his actual sentiments, rather than a pastiche of the language of the past. In many ways his poetry resembles that of Kotomichi. Both men chose to write about their own experiences and beliefs, rather than about the conventionally admired subjects, and both men led lives of self-imposed poverty, enjoying little recognition outside their own circles. But Akemi's subjects went beyond those found in the sphere of his house and garden, and his poetry has a coarse vigor foreign to Kotomichi. Many of his poems reveal a crude humor. He was involved with prostitutes and used the experiences gained from these relationships in his poetry:

Snow at a Brothel

niwa no yuki	Young ladies
tawaremarogasu	Having fun rolling
otomedomo	snowballs
sono te wa tare ni	With the garden snow,
nukumesasuran	Who will warm for you
	Your cold little hands?

Looking at Snow with a Woman

imo to ware	My sweetheart and I,
negao narabete	Sleepy face side by side,
oshidori no	Look out at the pond
ukiiru ike no	Covered with snow and
yuki wo miru kana	watch
	The mandarin ducks
	floating.

Akemi's sardonic comments, unlike Kotomichi's, were usually directed not at lovable little foibles but at pretension, vulgarity, and conventional kinds of poetry:

itsuwari no	Don't write clever poems
takumi wo iu na	Compounded out of
makoto dani	falsehoods—
sagureba uta wa	As long as they seek
yasukaran mono	Sincerity, your poems
	Will be easy to compose.

Akemi's most appealing *waka* are those in which he described his ordinary daily life. Although the language he used was old-fashioned at times, the sentiments were not, as can be illustrated by the following poem:

tanoshimi wa	It is a pleasure
mare ni uo nite	When we have fish for
kora mina ga	dinner,
umashi umashi to	A rare treat,
iite kuu toki	And my kids, crying,
	"Yum, yum!"
	Gobble it down.

With Akemi the *waka* had indeed acquired a contemporary content, as the poets had urged for years, but it had lost almost everything else. The traditional qualities of the *waka*—tone, overtones, evocation of mood—had been sacrificed in the interest of sincere expression. It is interesting to speculate what might have happened to the *waka* if Western influence had not flooded Japan the very year Akemi died. Perhaps one more "rediscovery" of the *Kokinshū* would have restored to the *waka* its traditional qualities, but more likely the impatience with the old poetic diction and narrow horizons, which Akemi displayed, would have taken roots elsewhere and led as surely to the disintegration of the old *waka* as the much-acclaimed revolution of the Meiji poets.

NOTE

1. Names ending in -hachi or -bei were typical of men living in Kotomichi's times, as opposed to names that were typical of court poets of the past.

Tanjirō and Ochō

TAMENAGA SHUNSUI

1790–1843

The principal form of literature in Japan today is undoubtedly the form of fiction called *shōsetsu*. The definition of *shōsetsu*, however, has become increasingly uncertain in recent years, now that non-fictional or openly autobiographical works are also considered to be *shōsetsu*. The term *shōsetsu*, though usually translated as "novels," includes not only works of novel length, but short stories and novellas. Since the term *shōsetsu* is used to embrace such different works, it would seem logical to use it also for *The Tale of Genji* or *The Tale of the Heike*, but Japanese critics normally do not refer to such works of classical literature as *shōsetsu*. The first *shōsetsu* are believed to have been written in Japan in the wake of Tsubouchi Shōyō's *Shōsetsu Shinzui* (The Essence of the Novel), but as a matter of fact, the term was first used in Japan in 1754 to designate works of fiction translated or adapted from

Chinese colloquial literature. In later years, however, the term *shōsetsu* came to be used generally for almost any kind of fiction.

Readings in colloquial Chinese literature, especially such erotic novels as *Chin P'ing Mei*, seem to have first suggested the possibility of using colloquial Japanese for literary purposes. One Confucian scholar wrote, "It is hard to describe real feelings accurately if you use the classical language, just as it is harder to write about daily life in *waka* than in a *haikai* verse. Rarely does anyone succeed. Writers can convey the emotions more easily and accurately if they write their novels in colloquial language. *The Tale of Genji* and *The Tales of Ise* are written in the classical language; that is why, even though they are erotic in content, they do not convey feelings as successfully as contemporary plays or popular fiction."

It was certainly unconventional to rate *The Tale of Genji* less highly than contemporary works, but the writer was surely on the right track when he stated that the emotions of the characters seem much more vivid when expressed in the colloquial than in the classical language. The use of the colloquial up to this time, whether in novels or plays, had generally been haphazard or even unintentional. A writer sometimes inadvertently included colloquial expression in his text, but the characters in the novels of Saikaku or Ueda Akinari do not use contemporary colloquial language. Even the *sewamono* of Chikamatsu, although based on current happenings, are written in a conventional stage language that only intermittently approaches the true colloquial. But in the *shōsetsu* written under the influence of colloquial Chinese fiction, the speech of the characters is extremely close to contemporary language.

The fiction of the latter part of the 18th and first half of the 19th centuries is usually known as *gesaku*. The term was apparently used by the brilliant eccentric Hiraga Gennai (1728?–79) in reference to his play *Shinrei Yaguchi no Watashi* (The Miracle at Yaguchi Ferry; 1770). Gennai must have felt that it was beneath his dignity as a samurai to write a work for the theater, and therefore described his work as *gesaku*, meaning a "playful composition." This had nothing to do with the content of this work, which is a historical tragedy, but with the attitude of the author. By pretending he wrote the play in an idle moment, Gennai maintained a suitable distance from his own creation, acting the part of a dilettante who disclaimed responsibility for a work never intended to be taken seriously.

By the end of the 18th century the term *gesaku* was used for works of fiction ranging from books of cartoons to immensely long novels that extolled the Confucian virtues. The readers similarly ranged from near-illiterates to members of the imperial court. *Gesaku* fiction began with the *sharebon*, a kind of humorous writing that first appeared about 1745. It borrowed its format from Chinese erotic books, and often included a preface in mock-Chinese and Chinese-looking titles, as if to establish the ties between this new literature and Chinese colloquial fiction. The contents, however, were purely Japanese. A *sharebon* was usually devoted to describing the manners, clothes, and styles of speaking of the customers and prostitutes of the pleasure quarters, evoking realistic scenes in Edo or Kyoto.

The writers of these books were mainly samurai. They justified their taste for frivolity by asserting that they were following the tradition of Chinese gentlemen who were able, thanks to their indulgence in women and wine, to scale the heights of poetry.

Although the authors were educated men, these books were totally lacking in intellectual content. On the other hand, they are surprisingly non-erotic; there is almost no suggestion of what was, after all, the main business of the pleasure quarter. A brothel was described as a kind of club whose members were more interested in observing and commenting on one another than in lying with the prostitutes. A *sharebon* is like a manual of pleasure-quarter etiquette, providing examples of the appropriate banter between customers and prostitutes. Occasionally, as in *Keisei-kai*

Shijūhatte (The Forty-Eight Grips in Buying a Whore; 1790) by Santō Kyōden (1761–1816), such banter is filled with sensuality and even rises to the level of literature:

> Woman (*peeping into Customer's face*): Oh, dear! He's fallen asleep, has he? Wake up! Wake up! (*She blows smoke into his face.*)
> Customer (*choking from the smoke*): I didn't sleep a wink all night. (*He dozes off again.*)
> Woman: I won't stand for it. You're not going to sleep if I can help it. You can sleep tonight. Come on, open your eyes, open them. (*She tweaks his nose.*)

Such passages were presumably the reason for the order issued in 1791 confining Kyōden to his house in manacles for fifty days because his writings were reportedly indecent.

The Kansei Reforms, the collective name for the edicts issued by the senior councillor Matsudaira Sadanobu between 1789 and 1793, in an attempt to restore the dignity and importance of the samurai class, were responsible for Kyōden's misfortune, but the encouragement of education provided by the Kansei Reforms led to a great increase in the potential readers of fiction. The number of lending libraries markedly grew, and their patrons included a conspicuously large number of women and that, no doubt, is why much of the later *gesaku* fiction was aimed at women. The writing of fiction became more and more of a commercial enterprise. In place of samurai tossing off *gesaku* for the amusement of their friends, the new authors tried to appeal to as wide an audience as possible in order to enhance their income from royalties. This development created a much more solid base of readers for the new *gesaku* than for the old. Today only specialists read the works of Santō Kyōden, but *Tōkai Dōchū Hizakurige* (Travels on Foot along the Eastern Sea Highway; 1802–22), *Ukiyoburo* (The Up-to-date Bathhouse; 1809–13), and *Umegoyomi* (Plum Calendar; 1832–33) are part of the common literary heritage.

Travels on Foot and *The Up-to-date Bathhouse* are entertaining mainly because of their amusing situations and conversations, but they possess little novelistic interest. They lack plot or structure, but consist of almost unrelated episodes linked either by the same characters or by the same locale (for example, a public bath). *Plum Calendar*, by contrast, is a novel. The *ninjōbon*, of which *Plum Calendar* is the finest example, developed from the *sharebon*, but instead of being a guide to the pleasure quarters, it was about love. The hero was no longer the connoisseur who is admired for his perfect knowledge of pleasure-quarter etiquette, but a handsome young man whose chief distinction is his magical attraction for many women. It would have been the height of boorishness for the hero of a *sharebon* to fall in love, but in a *ninjōbon* the hero not only fell in love but even married. He, like all the other characters in the book, was provided by the author with a distinct personality. No longer was the dialogue identified merely as being between a customer and a prostitute; the names of the speakers are always given. The hero of a *ninjōbon* was a man for whom women were eager to make sacrifices. He was generally incapable of earning a living and was not ashamed to take money from his adoring girl-friends. He was a master of the art of making love, but was otherwise rather effeminate, and if attacked by a villain was likely to fall an easy victim. But this did not disillusion the women in his life. Far from it: the weaknesses of the hero made them love him all the more.

The *ninjōbon* were aimed mainly at women of the samurai or upper merchant class, who derived their greatest pleasure from Kabuki and desired the same atmosphere in the books they read. They craved above all books whose heroines were women with whom they could identify themselves: women who were passionately devoted to their lovers, generous to their friends, and always ready to sacrifice their own happiness. These readers did not object to suggestions of physical intimacy between the hero and the heroines, but they were shocked by overt descriptions. The *nin-*

jōbon were accordingly erotic, but rarely pornographic.

The authors of the *ninjōbon* constantly made their presence felt in the stories. They appear as friendly and understanding observers who from time to time make comments for the edification of the readers. This was true especially of Tamenaga Shunsui. Shunsui was not the originator of the *ninjōbon*, but he certainly raised it to its highest level. He was born into a merchant family in Edo and apparently studied with professional *gesaku* writers as a young man, but almost nothing is known about his early life. He founded a publishing company in 1821, but, lacking the money or authority to attract new writers, he brought out old works by established authors without paying them. The enraged reactions of these authors can easily be imagined. Perhaps that is why Shunsui turned to publishing his own books.

Shunsui's early works, as he later confessed, were written mainly by assistants. It is possible, however, that he wrote them himself and pretended they were the work of assistants in order to disassociate himself from their clumsiness. He had written about thirty *ninjōbon*, with or without assistance, by 1832, when the first parts of his masterpiece, *Plum Calendar*, started to appear. When completed the following year, it had become the most enjoyable work of nineteenth-century Japanese fiction, at least before Futabatei Shimei's *Ukigumo* (The Drifting Cloud; 1887–89).

Plum Calendar consists mainly of conversations together with brief introductory passages, *togaki* (stage directions), and occasional comments by the author. The central role of dialogue and *togaki* is a clear indication of the influence of Kabuki on Shunsui's writings. Most of the novel is in the colloquial. It has often been said that *The Drifting Cloud* was the first Japanese novel written in the colloquial, but in reality, fifty years earlier *Plum Calendar* had earned this distinction. The language is at times startlingly close to modern Japanese, and the novel as a whole is a bridge between the literature of the past and the works of such modern authors as Nagai Kafū.

Plum Calendar is the story of Tanjirō, the illegitimate son of a high-ranking gentleman. He is falsely implicated in the theft of a valuable heirloom and, being unable to prove his innocence, he goes into hiding. The book opens as Yonehachi, a geisha in love with Tanjirō, makes her way to his hideout. Gradually we learn of her passionate devotion to him and of the fierce jealousy she displays towards any other woman in his life. She wants the sole privilege of supplying him with money, cooking his meals, and sharing his bed. Another girl, Ochō, with whom Tanjirō grew up, almost as brother and sister, is also in love with him, though he denies this to Yonehachi.

One of the best scenes in the novels relates how Tanjirō and Ochō accidentally meet in the street. He invites her into a restaurant where she unabashedly reveals her love. Like Yonehachi, she desires nothing more than to provide for him. Tanjirō, being reluctant to disclose his relations with Yonehachi, urges Ochō to be more cautious. Ochō suspects he must have another sweetheart, and at once becomes jealous. Tanjirō, to change the subject, opens the window and looks out on the street. At this moment Yonehachi passes and catches a glimpse of Tanjirō. He is acutely embarrassed to be caught between the two women he loves, and tries to leave before Yonehachi can reach him. At this point (the end of the chapter), Shunsui addresses an aside to the readers: "What will be the emotions of Tanjirō and Ochō when they go down the stairs and meet Yonehachi? The author still hasn't thought of a good solution. . . . If any readers have good suggestions to make, I beg them to get in touch with the author at once."

The next chapter follows immediately on the previous scene. The two rivals for Tanjirō's love meet and drink together. Yonehachi declares that although she is a geisha she considers herself to be Tanjirō's wife. Ochō, no less determined, insists that she will henceforth provide for Tanjirō. The two women exchange sarcasms until Tanjirō, who has thus far been listening passively, announces he will show Ochō home. Yonehachi pinches his back fiercely and mutters, "Leave at once. I can't stand you." Tanjirō answers with a grim smile, "You're crazy. You're too much for me." "So I'm crazy, am I?" cries Yonehachi, throwing down the toothpick from between her teeth. She adds in a soft voice, "You'd better take Ochō by the hand so she doesn't get lost."

Plum Calendar is wonderfully effective in such scenes and deserves the popularity it enjoyed. It indeed proved so popular that it was expanded to twice the originally planned length with no great harm to the plot. No doubt it titillated the women readers, especially when Ochō and Tanjirō finally make love, but Shunsui defended himself from the charge of immorality: "In general, I write my books with the expectation that most of the readers will be women; that is why they are so crude and clumsy. But even though the women I portray may seem immoral, they are all imbued with deep sentiments of chastity and fidelity. I do not write about women who have affairs with many men, or who indulge in lustful pursuits for the sake of money, or who deviate from the true path of morality, or who are wanting in wifely decorum. There are many romantic passages in this book, but the feelings of the men and women I have described are pure and uncorrupted."

Shunsui wrote many other *ninjōbon*, some almost as successful as *Plum Calendar*. At the end of 1841, however, he was summoned to a magistrate's office and questioned about his books. In the spring of 1842 he was put in manacles for fifty days, and his illustrator and publishers were fined for having been associated with Shunsui's immoral books. The blocks for the books were destroyed, and bound volumes were burned. Shunsui died in 1843, no doubt weakened by the shock of this punishment.

The *ninjōbon* were revived after the Tempō Reforms ended, but they did not achieve the excellence of *Plum Calendar*. The influence they exerted on the creation of modern Japanese literature, however, was greater than that of any other form of Kinsei writing, and *Plum Calendar* is the one book of the late Tokugawa period I can read today with unmixed pleasure.

HIRATA ATSUTANE

1776–1843

The pleasures of Kinsei literature are not confined to the usual literary genres of poetry, fiction, and drama. Among the most enjoyable works are the *zuihitsu*—musings by scholars on different occasions on the origins of a special custom or nomenclature, his accounts of men of unusual virtue or wickedness, and his reminiscences about old friends, all indiscriminately joined together with no semblance of order. *Zuihitsu* were not meant for readers who desired a logical exposition of a theory or the development of a plot. They were intended to be read as casually as they were written, but in the end they provide the materials for a kind of autobiography without chronology. Although the *zuihitsu* author rarely gives a coherent account of his own life or beliefs, we can infer from his jottings much about the man and about his time.

Some works of criticism or philosophy are also as pleasurable as literature. Motoori Norinaga was not only a great critic but he also wrote so skillfully that his works make absorbing reading. His disciple Hirata Atsutane was not so literarily gifted, and his writings are moreover colored by a nationalistic bias which is so extreme at times as to become comic. His assertions that all the other nations of the world when compared to Japan are base and contemptible are hard to accept at face value, but they provide extraordinary insights into the way of thinking of a man who was born in the year of the American Revolution and died just five years before the many European revolutions of 1848 changed the course of modern history.

Hirata always styled himself a disciple of Motoori, but he never met Motoori and entered his school only after his death. Fortunately, however, Motoori appeared to Hirata in a dream and formally accepted him as a pupil, reciting two *waka* to celebrate the occasion. Later, Hirata established himself as the leading *kokugaku* scholar of his day. His publications included not only works expounding the ancient Japanese way, but also intemperate attacks on Chinese civilization and bitter anti-Buddhist tracts. Hirata was by no means scrupulous in his choice of weapons when fighting ideological enemies. He artfully chose scurrilous details from the Buddhist canon to discredit Shakyamuni Buddha, at one point deriding him as a *kurombō* (black man) because some scholars thought he was born in Colombo. Hirata asserted, similarly, that cloves and other spices were grown in India and Indonesia to have means of mitigating the foul odor emitted by the inhabitants.

Hirata, however, did not deny that a knowledge of foreign countries could be useful to Japan. He declared that Shinto learning was much deeper and wider than either Confucianism or Buddhism, likening it to a great sea into which all the other varieties of learning emptied themselves. He sometimes wrote disparagingly about Westerners, comparing them to animals, and even reporting that they lifted one leg when urinating, just like dogs. But he greatly admired certain aspects of Western learning, notably

astronomy. He was especially interested in the moon because he believed (perhaps under European influence) that the moon and the earth were once joined. At that time men freely passed from the earth to the moon after they died, but after the moon separated from the earth, it no longer could serve as *yomi*, the world of the dead. When he was informed that the Europeans had invented a telescope so powerful that men and horses could be detected on the moon, he at once wrote his son to confirm this rumor.

Hirata was fascinated by all varieties of supernatural phenomena. His work *Kokon Yōmikō* (A Study of Weird Beings, Ancient and Modern; 1828) consists of evidence of the supernatural drawn from many sources, together with Hirata's explanations. He was especially intrigued by *tengu*, winged goblins of Japanese folklore. One can imagine therefore with what excitement Hirata learned in 1820 of a boy who claimed he had been taken to the moon by a *tengu*. His work *Senkyō Ibun* (Strange Tidings from the Realm of the Immortals) opens in this manner: "At seven o'clock on the evening of the first day of the tenth month of 1820, old man Yashiro Waike called on me and reported that a boy now at Yamazaki Yoshishige's house had been lured off by the *tengu* and, after spending many years with them, had now come as their messenger. Yashiro said that the boy had much to say about what he had seen and heard, and that the boy's descriptions agreed in many ways with what I had previously thought and written. He added that he was about to go to Yamazaki's place to see the boy and asked me if I would not go along. I was delighted to do so, since I am always eager to meet such persons and question them about various matters."

On the way Hirata was told that the boy, unlike similar individuals who claimed to have visited the "other world" but gave vague and confusing accounts, talked readily about his experiences. The boy declared that he had traveled even to countries at the distant western end of the world, and imitated the cries of a Persian bulbul he had heard. The boy said that he had previously been forbidden to reveal anything about the other world to people of this world. But of late he had been told by his master that it was no longer necessary to conceal anything. He urged people he met to ask questions freely and to record his answers before they forgot them. Hirata, hearing this, reasoned that many other kinds of information which had formerly been secret—whether about this world, the gods, or foreign countries—had gradually become known in recent times, and it was therefore not surprising that the time had also come for facts about the realm of the *tengu* to be divulged.

When Hirata and his friend first met the boy at Yamazaki's house, he merely stared at them. Only at Yamazaki's insistence did the boy finally execute a bow, and it was very clumsy. The boy was said to be fifteen but Hirata thought he looked more like thirteen. His eyes were his most striking feature. They were unusually large and flashed penetratingly as he gazed at the visitors. Hirata, a doctor, took the boy's pulse and felt his abdomen. There was surprising strength in the abdomen, but the boy's pulse was extremely faint, like that of a six- or seven-year-old child. Hirata was told that the boy was called Torakichi because he had been born in the year of the tiger (*tora*) on the day and hour of the tiger.

From the time Torakichi was five or six, he had possessed an ability to predict future events. For example, on the day before a devastating fire at Shitaya Hirokōji he climbed to the roof of his house and cried out that there was a fire. Nobody else could detect any signs of a fire, and the boy was asked why he had said such a foolish thing. Torakichi answered, "You mean you can't see the fire, even when it's burning that way? We should run away!" People thought he was out of his mind, but the next night, true to his prophecy, Hirokōji was destroyed by a fire. On another occasion he warned his father that he would hurt himself the next day and urged him to be careful. The father, paying no attention to the boy, was careless and hurt himself badly.

Hirata was naturally eager to learn more, and Torakichi seemed equally impressed by Hirata. After carefully examining Hirata's face, Torakichi suddenly smiled and repeated several times, "You are a god." Hirata listened in speechless surprise, apparently not displeased by this revelation. The boy continued, "You believe and study the ways of the gods." Only then did Yamazaki reveal to the boy for the first time that Master Hirata was a scholar who taught the ancient Shinto learning. Torakichi said that he had guessed as much from Hirata's face.

Torakichi began to tell his story for the visitors' benefit, describing how his interest in the world of spirits was first aroused in 1812 when he was seven. He was intrigued by a fortuneteller who stood before the Inari Shrine in Ikenohata Kayamachi, and begged the old man to teach him the mysteries of his art. The old man said that Torakichi must first undergo the prescribed discipline of holding oil in the palm of his hand for seven days, then lighting it. The boy did as he was told but only succeeded in burning his hand; the old man still refused to divulge the mysteries.

The same year Torakichi encountered a man of about fifty with long hair who carried a small jar containing the medicine he sold. He told Torakichi that he himself was able to squeeze himself into the jar and presently did so, whereupon the jar flew off into the sky. The next day the old man reappeared at the same place and urged Torakichi to enter the jar with him, promising to teach him the secrets of telling fortunes. Torakichi, having been disappointed by such a promise before, hesitantly agreed, but soon went with the old man into the jar.

They were immediately transported to a mountain in Hitachi which, as Hirata noted, was known as a place where the *tengu* practiced their rituals. However, when it grew dark the boy missed his parents so badly that the old man agreed to allow him to return home, on condition that he must not disclose to anyone what he had seen. The boy agreed. The old man urged Torakichi to return the next day to the usual spot, again promising to teach him divination. Thereupon he took the boy on his back, told him to shut his eyes, and rose into the sky. There was a rushing noise in Torakichi's ears, and presently he found himself back home. The old man at once vanished. Torakichi, true to his promise, told no one what had happened. For the next five years, from the time he was seven to eleven, Torakichi accompanied the old man on his travels throughout the country. On one occasion he was taken to Iwama in Hitachi where he met his present master. This master refused to teach the boy divination, but guided him instead in the martial arts, calligraphy, and the secrets of both Shinto and Buddhism. Even though the boy sometimes stayed away from home for as long as one hundred days, no one ever noticed his absence.

When Torakichi was eleven his father fell gravely ill, and being worried about the boy's future, ordered him to become a Buddhist priest, since he seemed too frail for any other profession. The boy entered a temple where he quickly established a reputation as a worker of spells. In 1819, after the death of his father, the master reappeared and urged Torakichi to come with him. They went

again to Mount Iwama, and from there to Ise, where they worshipped both shrines. They returned three months later, only to
set out again, this time flying to China and other countries.

Hirata and his friends were fascinated by the boy's story and
arranged to see him again. When Torakichi visited Hirata's house
he was shown a stone flute, said to be a relic of the age of the gods,
and immediately began to play it. He was asked numerous questions about the other world. Hirata would ask, for example, if
there were guns in the other world, to which Torakichi replied
that the guns of the other world were similar to those in this
world, but one variety was loaded with wind. Torakichi also gave
a demonstration of the style of calligraphy he had learned on the
mountain, impressing even masters of the art by his skill.

Hirata was so reluctant to let the boy go before he had fully
examined him that when Torakichi announced his return to Mount
Iwama, Hirata addressed a formal letter to persons attending the
master of the world of the spirits asking permission for Torakichi

to continue his descriptions of the secrets of the other world.

Torakichi returned unexpectedly soon, and this time was accepted into the Hirata household. He was subjected to a detailed examination concerning not only his life among the mountain men and *tengu* but his visits to foreign countries. In response to the question, "Weren't there foreign countries where they worship something like a cross or pictures of a crucified man or pictures of a woman holding a small child in her arms?" Torakichi replied that he had visited a country "a very cold place where people wore splendid, narrow-sleeved clothes" and such images were worshiped. When he asked his master about them, he was told that these were the divinities of the false creed called Christianity. "In Japan this religion is strictly prohibited, so the master spat on them."

Torakichi's explanation of the relations between the gods and men was simple. "It goes without saying that the gods are free to do as they please. Just as men manipulate dolls, they manipulate men. Mountain men, *tengu*, and the like are close to the gods, and therefore do as they please. There is nothing to marvel at." However, contrary to the general impression among men, the mountain men never drink saké except at New Year because it befuddles the senses.

The most exciting part of Torakichi's account is his description of a visit to the moon. If we can believe his account, he was undoubtedly the first Japanese ever to come so close to the moon. Here is his description: "The closer one gets to the moon the bigger it appears. The cold was so intense it penetrated us, and it seemed impossible to go much closer, but we braved the cold and went to a distance of about two hundred yards, only to find to our surprise that it was quite warm there. The places at the moon's surface which seem to shine resemble seas on the earth and look as if they contain some mud. At the place which is popularly supposed to be where the rabbit pounds rice cakes[1], there were two or three holes, but we were some distance away, so I could not ascertain the condition precisely."

Surprised, Hirata asked, "The Westerners also have the theory that the shining parts of the moon are like the seas on earth, and I can well believe this is true, but it is hard to understand that there are holes at the place where a rabbit seems to be pounding rice cakes. I wonder if they are not like the mountains on earth."

Torakichi replied with a smile, "Your theories come from books, and that's why they are wrong. I don't know about books. I have merely told you what I saw when I was close by. There were without question two or three holes, and stars were visible through the holes on the other side of the moon. There is no doubt about the holes."

Hirata's account of his conversations with Torakichi run to over two hundred double-columned pages. Nowhere does he suggest any doubts about the authenticity of the boy's statements. But it would be unfair to treat Hirata simply as a gullible, ignorant man. He was well-educated in Japanese learning and even had some acquaintance with Western science. Moreover, he was not alone in being impressed by Torakichi. Learned old gentlemen listened with awe to the boy's descriptions of the other world. It is still a mystery to me how Torakichi managed to keep inventing new details of his life among the *tengu*, even to drawing pictures of their weapons and examples of their writing. I cannot believe the boy actually traveled with a *tengu* to China, Europe, and the moon, but I must admit that he was indeed a child prodigy.

Once Torakichi had told his tale, however, there was not much else for him to do. After living in the Hirata household for some years he resumed his old profession of Buddhist priest, despite all his unkind remarks about Buddhism in his interviews. It is easy to imagine Hirata's shock and disappointment at this decision.

Senkyō Ibun is in no sense a literary masterpiece, but it makes constantly absorbing reading. It is a pity it is accessible now only in the *Complete Works of Hirata Atsutane*. It provides the reader with an unforgettable glimpse of a seldom-revealed side to life in the Japanese intellectual world at the end of the Kinsei period.

NOTE

1. Japanese have long imagined that they could see a rabbit pounding rice cakes (*mochi*) in the configurations of the moon, much as people in the West imagine they can see a man's face.

THE MEIJI PERIOD (1868–1912)

The Meiji period covers the years between 1868, when the capital was moved from Kyoto to Tokyo and the youthful emperor chose the name Meiji for his reign, and 1912, when he died.

Many of the samurai who had fought the shogunate troops in order to restore power to the emperor had been extremely xenophobic. It might have been supposed that the new regime would therefore break all ties with foreign countries, but in fact the opposite occurred. Most xenophobes shifted almost without transition from uncritical hatred of the West to uncritical admiration for all aspects of Western civilization. Translations of European works—not only of literature but of a technical nature—spurred young Japanese to make their country as much like a Western nation as possible. The period of uncritical admiration lasted until about 1885, but even after it ebbed Western influence continued to affect Japanese life in innumerable ways. Western influence can be detected even in works of this period that seem most faithful to the old Japanese traditions, but it was a rediscovery of the importance of these traditions in the late 1880s which helped to save modern Japanese literature from becoming nothing more than a provincial offshoot of European literature. The writers of the 1890s especially prepared the ground for the extraordinary flowering of Japanese writing of the twentieth century.

ŌNUMA CHINZAN

1818–1891

Probably the earliest work of Meiji literature was *Tōkei shi sanjisshu* (Thirty Poems on Tokyo), a collection of thirty *shichigen zekku* (quatrains in seven character lines) by Ōnuma Chinzan, published in 1869. Today, this work is almost unknown. Even the novelist and antiquarian Nagai Kafū, who wrote a long account of Chinzan's life, supposed that the *kanshi* written by Chinzan which describe the beginning of the new era had been lost. The publication in 1943 of *Meiji Shiwa* (Chats on Meiji Chinese Poetry) by Kinoshita Hyō included Chinzan's unique work and made it available again. In Chinzan's poems the humorous and sometimes sardonic comments of the rapid changes taking place are described as seen through the eyes of a gentleman-scholar of the old school.

Chinzan was fifty years old when the name Edo was officially changed to Tōkei.[1] Soon afterwards the *nengō* (reign name) Keiō was changed to Meiji, and early in November the imperial palanquin left Kyoto for the new capital, where it arrived three weeks later. Naturally the excitement in Tōkei was enormous. The first poem in Chinzan's collection relates:

> The Son of Heaven has moved his capital and bestowed his largesse;
> The boys and girls of Tōkei look as lovely as flowers.
> Observe how "Duck Waters" has lost out to "Seagull Crossing;"[2]
> Quite a few nobles no longer think about home.

The mention of "largesse" doubtless refers to the distribution of saké to the populace in the eleventh month in celebration of the emperor's arrival. "Duck Waters" refers to the Kamo River in Kyoto, and "Seagull Crossing" to the Sumida River. The poem thus indicates that now that the capital has been moved and the Kyoto nobles are about to rule the country after taking over from the deposed Tokugawa regime, they have forgotten about their old homes in Kyoto.

The nobles were not the only men to feel the lure of the new capital. Once the feudal restrictions on travel had been lifted, many ambitious men from all over Japan flocked to Tokyo in the hopes of making their fortunes there. On the other hand, samurai who had been associated with the former Tokugawa regime left the city, some to follow the last shogun, Tokugawa Keiki, to Shizuoka, others to seek employment in the countryside. By the end of 1868 a new component was added to the population of Tokyo. Foreigners, hitherto restricted to Yokohama and other port cities, were permitted to reside in the Tsukiji section of Tokyo. Horse carriages, imported from abroad, carried the foreigners to and from Yokohama, and before long the Japanese nobles and officials, not to be outdone, also adopted this swift-moving conveyance. Chinzan's second poem describes the change:

Paired horses pull the carriages bearing the great men;
They pass in the flash of an eye over the city streets.
P'an Yüeh would have had no way to gaze worshipfully at
 their dust—
They rush by like stars and lightning in a moment's time.

The third line refers to the servile P'an Yüeh who bowed in
reverence towards the dust stirred up by the nobles' carriages.
Chinzan meant to say that with this new way of traveling, such
old-fashioned gestures would be impossible because of the speed
of the horse carriages.

There is a note of strong conservative disapproval in Chinzan's
poems. Because he had lived comfortably under the old regime,
he understandably tended to deplore any changes. Although the
end of the Tokugawa period had been turbulent, he himself had
led the life of a *bunjin* of the past, a life which included the enjoy-
ment of saké and moon-viewing. Kafū noted, for example, that
at the time of the harvest moon in 1844, Chinzan, as was his
custom, went to admire the moon over the Sumida River. It was
rare to find a poem in Chinzan's *kanshi* of this time which did not
mention saké, the indispensable accompaniment to moon-viewing
and similar pleasures. But after the Meiji Restoration, when the
whole country was engaged in modernization, there was no time
to gaze at the moon or to enjoy a leisurely cup of saké. Kafū commented, "When I read his poems I realize that the highest delight
for the poets of Edo long ago was to admire the moon." No
wonder Chinzan resented the change in his life!

Chinzan was not a political poet. Unlike other *kanshi* poets who
voiced their indignation over the Opium War, or the arrival of
Commodore Perry's fleet, or the concessions made by the shogunate to the foreign powers, Chinzan rarely expressed either
anger or apprehension. In 1845 Yanagawa Seigan, the outstanding
kanshi poet of Edo, left the city as a gesture of disapproval of the
shogunate, but Chinzan remained behind. As Kafū noted, he had

come to lead Edo poetry-making circles by the ear. One of Ōnuma Chinzan's poems written about this time was called "Spring Regrets:"

> In the glorious days of Bunka and Bunsei
> Talented men excelled and each one gained fame.
> In word and deed fine compositions were esteemed;
> The judges of literary excellence were clear-seeing.
> Above and below all had the wealth they needed;
> In dealings with others men showed the sincerity in their
>   hearts.
> The country shone like the full moon,
> More than capable of preserving what had been achieved.
> One's ears heard only song and music;
> One's eyes saw no armored soldiers.
> The favor from above extended even to flowers and trees;
> Famous estates vied in the glory of spring.
> The city remains the same, but the people I knew are gone:
> And I too feel as old as the fabled Ting Ling Wei.

It is strange that Chinzan should have looked back so nostalgically to the Bunka and Bunsei eras (1804–29), as if those had been truly glorious times, though they are usually depicted in modern histories as a period of corruption and institutional decay. Kafū, who identified himself with Chinzan and noted the parallels in their lives, had the same longing for the past. At a time when public sentiment in favor of reverence for the emperor and expulsion of foreigners was growing more intense each day, Chinzan remembered affectionately the pleasant life of the past. Kafū sensed that people's motives for action had become even more hateful and selfish ever since the Great Earthquake of 1923, an event which seemed to Japanese of the 1920s as much of a watershed of Japanese history as the Meiji Restoration, and it seemed to him that social decency was steadily deteriorating. He found comfort in Chinzan's poetry, as in the following, written in 1854:

Do not seek the brush of Tu Mu when he described warfare,
But reexamine the poems of Yüan-ming on drinking saké.
In a little room hang curtains and warm old deeds:
The remains of the cask, unfinished books—that is life.

Chinzan, as this poem suggests, managed to stay aloof from the turbulent events preceding the Meiji Restoration, composing Chinese poetry as before, enjoying his quiet pleasures. But after the Restoration his tone was often sarcastic:

A full head of lacquer-black hair falls to cover his shoulders;
He dismounts before a shop near a weeping willow.
The young girl, recognizing him at a glance, gives him a smile;
His umbrella is bat-like, his cape like a kite.

The samurai, Chinzan is saying, have now let their hair grow so long that it falls to their shoulders, and they now wear or carry elements of Western dress. Unlike the samurai visitors to the *yūkaku* (red-light district) of the past, this one is not ashamed to show his face, and he is welcomed as a regular customer. In 1869 the first foreign barbershop was opened in Tokyo, and the modish gentlemen of the day affected different hair styles, along with capes, silk hats, and Western-style umbrellas. These dandies included men who, but a few years earlier, had demanded that the shogunate expel the foreigners and had even risked their lives to this end. Once their side had gained victory, they abruptly changed their minds and now not only welcomed foreigners but aped them.

In the winter of 1870 the mansions of the daimyos in the Tsukiji area were demolished, and an enlarged residential area for foreigners, together with the new Shimabara red-light district, was opened on the site. Samurai were not permitted to wear swords when visiting either of these enclaves, but they used their weapons to guard the foreign ships tied up at the Tsukiji docks.

> A Little Yang-chou—that's the new Shimabara;
> Our browbeaten Japanese warriors guard the barbarian ships.
> "Please don't come here wearing your swords—
> Please bring me instead ten thousand coins."

Yang-chou, famed in Chinese poetry as a city of great prosperity, was mentioned by Chinzan to suggest how flourishing the new Shimabara licensed quarter was. But without money a man, even a samurai, is unwelcome; the last two lines are a prostitute's recommendation that her would-be customer come without swords but with plenty of cash.

Chinzan was especially sarcastic about the readiness of the samurai to take up foreign ways:

> Everyone has adopted the barbarian way of dress;
> Only sumo wrestlers and prostitutes still wear the old clothes.

He concluded that only the strongest and weakest members of Japanese society could resist change and maintain the old traditions. Chinzan himself refused to yield to the new ways. An account by the scholar of Chinese and theater critic Yoda Gakkai (1833–1909) of a publication party held in 1878 states that Chinzan still wore his hair in the old style, his forehead shaved and the rest of his hair gathered into a topknot.

Chinzan certainly was no advocate of *bummei kaika*. His attitudes, though often amusing, tend to be reactionary. When the old restrictions against Kabuki were lifted after the Restoration and samurai eagerly attended performances, not ashamed to be seen in the theater, Chinzan wrote this satirical quatrain:

> It is quite proper that the theaters attract nobles—
> The superb talents of master actors are all but divine!
> Who now will laugh at "monkeys wearing crowns?"
> Saruwaka Street is full of gentlemen these days.

The theaters had been concentrated in the Saruwaka district of

Asakusa ever since the Tempō Reforms of the 1830s. But the stigma attached to Kabuki had only now been removed. In 1877 the Emperor Meiji himself witnessed the famous Kabuki actors Danjūrō and Kikugorō perform. No doubt he was following the custom of European sovereigns who patronized the theater, but to a conservative like Chinzan this was deplorable.

Occasionally the tone of Chinzan's poems becomes bitter, as when he described the hardships of samurai who were obliged to take menial jobs in Tokyo after they lost their masters. *The Ricksha Man*, a poem in forty lines, begins:

> Ricksha boy, why up so early?
> To wipe the dust from my ricksha.
> My customers still haven't come,
> But I get up at dawn to be ready.
> "What did you do in the old days?"
> I was a shogunate man with three thousand *koku*.
> When I left my house I rode in a chair or on horseback,
> Proud to be a samurai of high rank.
> Today I have forgotten all that:
> I gladly carry a merchant in my ricksha.

In the latter part of the poem Chinzan contrasted the uprightness of this samurai, who would rather pull a ricksha than demean himself by toadying to the new masters of Japan, with the baseness of his former colleagues who have no such scruples. Chinzan identified himself with those who refused to be tempted by the new politics or standards of morality. In one poem Chinzan even praised women of the samurai class who had become prostitutes in order to support their indigent families.

Chinzan so deplored the changes brought in by the Meiji Restoration that he continued as late as 1878 to refer to his city as Edo. He sought consolation from his griefs in drink, and a disciple wrote that even until the time of his death Chinzan never foreswore his association with the saké cup. At the end of his life he became a figure of fun, mocked by people because he dressed in clothes that nobody wore any longer and because he still wore his hair in the style of the old regime. When he fell ill in 1891 (at the age of 73) he refused to take medicine, saying that he had lived long enough. He was right. He had outlived his time, and the world around him seemed sadly debased.

His poetry, written in classical Chinese, the language of the samurai intellectuals, was filled with a sharpness of observation rare in conventional *kanshi*. It is still enjoyable today and, most important, it provides us with our first glimpse of the new Japan.

NOTES
1. The city was known as Tōkei for several years before the present pronunciation, Tokyo, became universally accepted.
2. "Duck Waters" refers to the Kamo River in Kyoto because the name is the homonym of *kamo*, or "duck." "Seagull Crossing" refers to the Sumida River in Tokyo because of a poetic allusion.

KANAGAKI ROBUN

1829–1894

At the end of the Tokugawa Period the Japanese novel was at the lowest level in centuries. In the 1860s not one novel still remembered today was published. In Europe such varied works as *Alice in Wonderland, Crime and Punishment,* and *Thérèse Raquin* were appearing, but from Japan there was only silence. With rare exceptions the later *gesaku* writers had absolutely nothing to say. If they could have made a living in some other, equally undemanding manner, they no doubt would cheerfully have abandoned their profession. Their number, in any case, was incredibly small. In 1872 two leading *gesaku* writers, Kanagaki Robun and Jōno Arindo, presented a memorial to the Ministry of Instruction describing the history of *gesaku* and its possible value to a new, enlightened society. They stated that only two or three other men besides themselves were making a living as *gesaku* writers. Perhaps they exaggerated the sad state of the Japanese novel, but even a detailed list of novels published in Japan between 1860 and 1872 indicates that there were no more than ten active authors. By the time of the Meiji Restoration the annual production of *gesaku* consisted chiefly of continuations of extensive works begun years before.

Why, we may wonder, had *gesaku* fiction dropped to such an abysmal level? No doubt the "reign of terror" of the Tempō reforms (1841–43), when some leading *gesaku* authors were imprisoned or forbidden to write, inhibited literary production. By the end of the Tokugawa period, however, the *gesaku* authors were again free to treat their usual subjects, such as the activities of the *yūkaku*, but the potentialities of such subjects were already virtually exhausted. The *kokkeibon* (comic books) were so trivial, so deficient in the kind of wit that makes the writings of Jippensha Ikku and Shikitei Samba enjoyable even today, that they seem devoid of substance. The *gōkan* (bound volumes), stories of vendettas and supernatural occurrences, appealed mainly to the eye rather than to the mind. The illustrations in the texts attracted prospective purchasers by a display of virtuosity that all but defied the limitations of the woodcut, but the literary content could hardly have engrossed any but the least discerning readers.

The *ninjōbon*, which in Tamenaga Shunsui's hands had developed into the most appealing variety of *gesaku*, was vestigially preserved. Indeed, Shunsui's successor, a samurai who took the name Shunsui II, was busy continuing the *Iroha Bunko* (ABC Library), a work begun by Shunsui I in 1836. Shunsui II was chosen as the successor to the first Shunsui not because of his literary talent but because of his upright character, and he was obviously uncomfortable at writing *ninjōbon*. Unlike earlier writers who had given their grotesque or indecent novels a façade of respectability in order to escape rebuke from the censors, Shunsui II was a convinced believer in the principle of *kanzen chōaku* (encourage virtue and chastise vice), and only pretended to be interested in prostitutes and cutthroats. Thanks to his strict adherence to Confucian morality he converted the *ninjōbon* into an instrument for moral instruction, but as a writer he was a disaster.

The *gesaku* authors, unable to think up new twists to the old stories, resorted in desperation to compounding elaborate mélanges of disparate plots. The general conformity of Tokugawa society for decades at a time undoubtedly atrophied the imagination of the writers, and the closure of the country eliminated any possibility of stimulation from the outside world.

With the arrival of the foreigners after the Treaty of Shimoda the writers of fiction should have been provided with some striking new subjects, but only the most trivial or exotic details caught their attention. The *kawaraban* (tile editions) sold after the visit of Commodore Perry show him looking like the guardian deity of a Buddhist temple, his face framed by a fierce moustache and beard, his mouth opened in an imprecation. The accompanying texts on these broadsheets are no more than bare, garbled accounts of the circumstances of the arrival of the American fleet or else descriptions of the strange gifts brought from abroad. Even when the foreigners became fairly numerous, as a result of the opening of the ports, interest in them remained superficial. The artist Hashimoto Sadahide drew prints of the foreigners in Yokohama, and his book *Yokohama Kaikō Kembun Shi* (Record of Things Observed and Heard at the Open Port of Yokohama; 1861) is illustrated with caricatures of the foreign men, women, and children going about their daily activities in the foreign settlement. The foreigners in Yokohama, to judge by most accounts, were not an impressive lot. They consisted mainly of adventurers, sailors, women of doubtful reputation, and merchants drawn by the prospects of easy money. A British diplomat wrote, "Nowhere is there a greater influx, unless it be at some gold diggings, of the lawless and dissolute from all countries." It is strange, all the same, that the *gesaku* authors were not more intrigued by the foreigners in their midst, and that the readers, though living in an age of

great social change, should still have been satisfied with variations on the story of Yaoya Oshichi.

The leading *gesaku* author of the late Tokugawa and early Meiji
periods was Kanagaki Robun, the son of an Edo fishmonger. Robun's father, despite his humble profession, was an educated man
with a taste for *haikai* poetry, and he fostered his son's literary
talents. Apparently he was too poor to keep the boy with him, so
he sent Robun to another shop as an apprentice. The boy spent
whatever money he earned on books, mainly *gesaku* fiction. This
interest in literature, unusual for an apprentice, eventually led to
his meeting *haikai* poets and *gesaku* writers. Before long he was
also initiated into the pleasures of the *yūkaku*. In 1844, at the age
of 15, Robun wrote his first work, an undistinguished pastiche of
earlier *gesaku* writings. His first success came in 1855, when he
wrote a *kawaraban* piece about the Great Earthquake and persuaded
the famous artist Kawanabe Gyōsai to illustrate it. It sold so well
that Robun produced an expanded version soon afterwards, mark-
ing the beginning of his career as a journalist.

In 1860, the year women were first allowed to ascend Mount Fuji,
Robun climbed the mountain and wrote *Kokkei Fuji Mōde* (Funny
Visit to Fuji), narrating his experiences and giving his account
topicality by mentioning the women he saw. The book is frivolous, and like other *gesaku* writers Robun devoted an inordinate
amount of space to the excretory processes, giving special pi-
quance to his account by describing the embarrassment of women
who wished to relieve themselves in private while making their
pilgrimage up Mount Fuji. He also introduced some *rashamen*,
prostitutes who sold themselves to the foreigners in Yokohama.
This was neither an indication of indignation over the fact that
Japanese women were forced to sell their bodies to foreign brutes,
nor was he commending such women for making the stay of
foreign guests more agreeable. His only concern was selling
books, and such unusual details were likely to attract a large
number of readers. The illustrations to *Funny Visit to Fuji* show

people attired in Western dress, and in other works by Robun we see steamboats and balloons. But the contents hardly differed from works written fifty years earlier. Robun, like other *gesaku* authors of that period, seems not to have realized that the intrusion of the West was destined to alter Japanese life profoundly. He treated the new importations as mere accessories to traditional life, rather like the tobacco introduced by the Portuguese three hundred years earlier.

In 1868 Robun began a new work, but by then there was almost no demand for *gesaku* fiction. The next year was even worse. Not only were no new novels published, but a professor at the Confucian Academy, Shōheikō, proposed that all vulgar books be burned, since they were of no benefit to the nation. The *gesaku* writers were under attack not only from their old enemies, the Confucian scholars, but from the advocates of Western learning like Fukuzawa Yukichi, who condemned *gesaku* literature as a waste of time. Fukuzawa's advocacy of Westernization made him the chief butt of the lampoons of *gesaku* writers, who were not only amused by the unfamiliar Western learning but tended to be reactionary in their social outlook, reflecting the tastes of uneducated readers.

Nakamura Keiu, another advocate of Westernization, was also unfriendly towards *gesaku* fiction. He composed documents entitled "Four Pernicious Effects of Collecting Novels" and "Ten Ways to Burn and Destroy Lascivious Books." The "four pernicious effects" were: people who enjoy novels will certainly not act like decent citizens; women who enjoy novels often suffer from bad reputations, and those who do not are usually unhealthy and die young; sons and younger brothers of people owning collections of novels may stealthily take to reading them, destroying their future prospects or impairing their health; and people who are fond of novels often contract tuberculosis. Nakamura Keiu urged rich men to purchase such books together with the blocks and burn them.

In face of this double attack from mutual enemies, the Confucian upholders of the old order and the advocates of Western learning, the only weapon of the *gesaku* writers was their humor. In 1870 Robun published the first two parts of *Seiyō Dōchū Hizakurige* (Journey on Foot to the West), completed in 15 parts in 1886. Robun borrowed the formula of the original *Tōkai Dōchū Hizakurige*. His heroes, Yaji and Kita, are the grandsons of the original travelers, and like their ancestors they are typical sons of Edo—short-tempered, lustful, quarrelsome, inept, yet somehow lovable. Unlike the original Yaji and Kita, however, their adversaries are not bumpkins in the roadside towns of Japan but the foreigners encountered by the heroes in many countries on their journey from Yokohama to London. The two men are accompanied on their travels by Tsūjirō, an interpreter with a shaky knowledge of English who is infatuated with everything he sees of the West.

The humor in *Seiyō Dōchū Hizakurige* is still intermittently effective, even though Robun's prejudices against foreigners, especially dark-skinned foreigners, are rather embarrassing. He derived his knowledge of the countries he described from such popular works as Fukuzawa Yukichi's *Seiyō Jijō* (Conditions in the West), but the book succeeds less because of the information incorporated from Fukuzawa than because of the endless predicaments in which Yaji and Kita get involved, either because of their total ignorance of foreign customs or because of their prejudice against anything un-Japanese. When they arrive in Ceylon, for example, they show the contempt for the natives that the original Yaji and Kita showed towards rustics they met on their journey, but this disdain is heightened by a conviction that these people are not even human beings. They hurl coconuts at the natives, and when Yaji is attacked he declares that if any black man raises his hand against a Japanese he will break the man's skinny shanks and bundle them into firewood. Kita joins Yaji and dares the black men to lift a finger against them. "I'll twist off

your heads and sell them to a *tadon-ya* (maker of charcoal balls)!"
he cries.

The humor in *Seiyō Dōchū Hizakurige* rarely rises above such
crudities, but Robun's next work *Aguranabe* (1871–2) is a small
masterpiece, the first work of Meiji fiction that can still be read
with pleasure today. The title suggests people sitting around a pot
of beef stew, the dish which had become a symbol of *bummei
kaika* (Enlightenment). Buddhist prohibitions on eating the flesh
of four-footed animals were now rejected as barbarous super-
stitions, and Fukuzawa Yukichi insisted that in order to improve
their physiques the Japanese must eat meat. This was Robun's
point of departure, and most of the monologues in *Aguranabe*
are satiric explanations of why the speaker is so fond of meat.
These monologues capture brilliantly the atmosphere of the
times. *Seiyō Dōchū Hizakurige* described scenes known to Robun
only from books, but *Aguranabe* depicts Tokyo during the early
years of Meiji with the vividness of actual observation. The work
provides amusing examples of how the enlightened views of men
like Fukuzawa trickled down to ordinary citizens.

Robun continued his merrymaking at the expense of Fukuzawa with the publication of *Kyūri-zukai* (The Use of Cucum-
bers), a pun on a work by Fukuzawa with an identically pronounced title that meant Illustrated Explanations of Natural
Principles. But it was about this time that the Ministry of Instruction issued three prescriptions which defined the purposes of literature. Robun sent a reply promising to change his style completely
and follow the three prescriptions to the letter. He declared that
he conceived his mission to be one of giving painless guidance to
the uneducated. *Gesaku* would become an instrument of the
educational policy of the new state, serving to inculcate respect for
the emperor and the other virtues advocated by the Ministry of
Instruction.

In July of 1872 Robun wrote a short work set in the palace of
the Dragon King under the sea in which he described how *bummei*

kaika had reached that kingdom. Robun's preface stated: "Although this little book is but the *gesaku* of a moment, written in my usual style, the attentive reader may gain from it one aspect of the Enlightenment. I have written in a deliberately inelegant style because I had to make the book easily intelligible even to farmboys and country wives. It is my hope as well as that of my colleagues that by writing such 'useless' books we can supplement the useful works. The reader will surely find, even in our idle words, a modicum of meaning. The Enlightenment should take pride that it possesses the discrimination not to reject popular fiction simply because it is considered to be vulgar."

In his last years Robun increasingly devoted himself to topical events. In 1879, for example, he published *Gurando-shi Yamato Bunshō* (Japanese Documents on Grant), a biography of President Grant who had visited Japan that year. Other writings were concerned with geishas, who in the Meiji period had assumed the importance of the great *tayū* (courtesans) of the past. To the end, however, he remained a *gesaku* writer, desirous only of amusing the public. When his particular brand of humor lost its ability to amuse, because of changes in readers' interests, Robun, who knew no other way to write, had no choice but to bow from the scene. It is unlikely he felt any resentment or even disappointment. For half a century he had singlehandedly maintained the *gesaku* traditions, and he must have sensed that this form of writing would not be welcome to a public which under European influence had come to take a far more serious view of the functions of literature.

KAWATAKE MOKUAMI

1816–1893

The literary form which was least affected by the Meiji Restoration was the drama. Translators and imitators of European novels and poetry were able to publish their books in small editions and wait for the public to catch up with their advanced literary tastes. Even though a work like *Shōsetsu Shinzui* (Essence of the Novel) by Tsubouchi Shōyō at first sold only a few hundred copies, it could be reprinted once people became aware of its importance. But the practical requirements of the theater were obviously quite different. The owner of a theater could not afford to wait for weeks or even months for a play to win public favor. If it did not succeed immediately he had to replace the play with a more popular one in order to pay the salaries of the actors. Experiments with new varieties of theater were already made in the early Meiji period, but they failed because the audiences were basically conservative, and there were too few enthusiasts of modern drama to meet the expenses of running a theater.

Kabuki was still very much alive at the time of the Restoration, thanks largely to Kawatake Mokuami, the one major literary figure whose works straddled the old as well as the new regime. Some plays written by Mokuami during the Meiji period are so faithful to the old traditions that it is hard to detect any changes, but others distinctly reveal the spirit of their times, either because they treat contemporary events, employ European techniques of materials, or glorify the virtues which the new government was desirous of promoting. Kabuki not only remained the most important form of drama during the Meiji period but was able to survive competition from more modern forms of theatrical entertainment, whether Western-style plays or films. The texts of the new Kabuki plays formed a distinctive element in modern Japanese literature because the prevailing sentiments, unlike those of the novel or poetry, were those of the old society, rather than of modern times. Meiji novelists and poets did not hesitate to turn their backs on the works of their predecessors, if only because of the wretched state of fiction and poetry at the time of the Restoration, but Kabuki was flourishing, and there was no reason to jettison so vital an art. It was difficult moreover for audiences brought up on Japanese theatrical traditions to give up the brilliance of spectacle, stylized but dramatically effective acting, the music and dance and other typical features of Kabuki in favor of plays performed by people who sat around a drawing room discussing their problems in unassertive, prosaic language.

It seems likely that if a genius like Ueda Akinari had miraculously appeared at the beginning of the Meiji period, the traditional styles of Japanese fiction might have lasted longer, and if Mokuami had not existed, Kabuki might well have disappeared as completely as *gesaku* fiction. But Mokuami, whose number and variety of plays are awesome, was more than a superior dramatist. He was the only man at the time of the Meiji Restoration who could have represented Japanese tradition without feeling a sense of inferiority before even his most accomplished rivals in the West.

Mokuami was born in 1836 in the heart of Edo. For generations his family had been wholesale fish merchants, but his father had changed profession and become a pawnbroker. The boy received only the minimal education necessary to keep the pawnshop accounts, but he was otherwise quite precocious. At the age of thirteen or fourteen he was disowned by his straitlaced father when he discovered that the boy was already amusing himself with geishas. The next few years Mokuami spent as a vagabond. His life among the lower classes, including criminal elements, would provide him with invaluable materials for his plays.

As a young man he studied Japanese dance but demonstrated little aptitude. His lessons had an unexpected consequence: his teacher introduced him to the backstage world of the Kabuki theater, and he became a pupil of the fifth Tsuruya Namboku. His name first appeared on playbills in 1835 when he was nineteen. Due to family obligations he was forced to leave the theater for a time, but in 1841 he returned to Kabuki and never left it again. During the long period of activity, until his death in 1893, he composed a total of 360 plays, long and short, including 130 *sewamono*, 90 *jidaimono* (period pieces) and 140 *shosagoto* (dance plays). Mokuami did not write every act of these plays and relied on assistants for much of the work. But he himself sketched the outlines for the entire works and bore the responsibility.

Mokuami's first great success came in 1854 when he wrote the play commonly known as *Shinobu no Sōda* for the actor Ichikawa Kodanji. Mokuami was obliged to write and rewrite the play three times in order to satisfy Kodanji, an actor of unprepossessing appearance and voice who well knew his own limitations. To please this actor, who had grown up in the Kamigata region, Mokuami included in the play passages accompanied by the music of the *jōruri* theater, associated with Osaka. The incorpora-

tion of this music in a play written for Kabuki actors was an in-
novation and invited favorable comments. Kodanji became aware
of the exceptional talent of this previously inconspicuous dramatist, and he began a collaboration which lasted until 1866, the year
of his death.

Mokuami wrote for Kodanji such *sewamono* as *Nezumi Kozō*
(The Rat Boy), *Izayoi Seishin* (The Loves of Izayoi and Seishin),
and *Sannin Kichisa* (The Three Kichisas), three of the best-known
plays of the Kabuki repertory. At the same time he was also writing for other actors for whom he created such famous works as
Benten Kozō. Almost all these plays deal with the lives of members
of the lower classes and have for their heroes thieves, blackmailers,
swindlers, prostitutes, and similar characters. These figures were
portrayed unsentimentally, but their exploits delighted the
audiences, who could more readily identify with them than with
the great heroes or villains of the distant past. Becoming a thief
may even have seemed a desirable way of life to some townsmen
caught in the throes of poverty and unable to escape their fates.

Mokuami's plays are filled with violence and unconcealed expressions of lust, but their effect is softened by the use of poetic
language. A scene which might be disagreeable to watch if performed realistically was given artistry by the stylized gestures and
the rhythm of the poetic dialogue. The plays are usually badly
constructed, sometimes consisting of two almost unrelated plots,
one in the tradition of the *jidaimono*, devolving on a stolen heirloom, the other a *sewamono* about the lives of ordinary people. But
despite the failings in construction, Mokuami's plays perform
superbly, and sometimes the writing reaches a high literary level.

Mokuami had no literary or social principles he wished to voice
in his plays, nor had he any intention of criticizing society. It is
hard to detect in his works any major change in outlook from the
beginning of his career until the end of the Tokugawa period, and
some critics assert that Mokuami remained the same until his
death. Some even condemn him as a timid moralist who unques-

tioningly submitted to the policies of the authorities. Perhaps this is so, but if Mokuami served the government, it was only indirectly. His first concern was with the actors for whom he wrote the plays and with the audiences on whose favor he depended.

The first new development in the Kabuki of the Meiji period was *katsureki* (living history). The term originated in 1878 with Kanagaki Robun, who sarcastically used this term to refer to the historical accuracy of a new play by Mokuami. The play, *Yumi Chigusa no Shigetō*, treating a celebrated incident in the warfare between the Minamoto and the Taira, was closer to the historical facts than previous plays on this subject, and the outfits worn by Ichikawa Danjūrō IX and the other actors were faithful to the late Heian period costumes. Mokuami did not enjoy writing *katsureki* for Danjūrō. When he created *Hōjō Kudai Meika no Isaoshi* (1884) he complained of feeling so constricted by the historical facts that he could not write a decent Kabuki play, but Danjūrō insisted, and Mokuami had no choice but to comply. The performance was staged in as untraditional a manner as possible in order to persuade the spectators that they were watching real people and events. It is easy to imagine the discomfort of a 68-year-old man, who had spent a whole lifetime in the Kabuki theater learning its conventions and special techniques, suddenly being faced with the necessity of abandoning his skills in order to meet the demands of an actor. But such was the position of the playwright in the Meiji period.

Even while Mokuami was composing *katsureki* for Danjūrō, he was writing quite different plays for the fifth Kikugorō. These plays were called *zangirimono* (cropped hair plays), referring to the foreign haircuts adopted by the Japanese after the Restoration. They deal with contemporary events, especially those related to the *bummei kaika*. The characters not only wear Western clothes but speak familiarly of Western innovations like banks, railways, post offices, and diamond rings, and the sets were illuminated by gas lamps. Mokuami's *zangirimono* deliberately exploited the characteristics of the new age, however distasteful they may have seemed to a conservative man who was too old to change much after the Restoration. He was above all a craftsman, and for that reason it was probably easier for him to write *zangirimono*, which at least allowed him to give free rein to his imagination, than the *katsureki* plays which insisted on historical facts. When writing about the Meiji period, Mokuami would walk the streets of Tokyo observing people and the new ways of life. These observations enabled him to impart authentic details to the *zangirimono*, though at heart these plays were as old-fashioned as Mokuami himself in that they incorporated a lot of the traditional elements. His use of the old poetic language in passages accompanied by the samisen emphasized the contrast between the modernity of the subject and the conservatism of the approach.

Mokuami's first *zangirimono* was called *Tōkyō Nichinichi Shimbun*. It was neither an artistic nor a financial success, but it was the first Kabuki play to portray the Meiji period. The play was staged at the newly constructed Morita Theater in October of 1873. The basic plot, a tale of murder and revenge, differs little from those of the *bakumatsu* (late Tokugawa) period, but the characters and situations are new. The central character is a *rōnin* named Jinnai who has led a dissolute life ever since the end of the feudal regime deprived his life as a samurai of its meaning. One day a prosperous townsman named Hanzaemon, a man known for his charitable deeds, accidentally overhears a young couple planning to commit suicide because of their desperate financial plight. He gives them seventy yen so that they can survive their difficulties. After the couple depart, Jinnai drunkenly stumbles onto the scene and kills Hanzaemon for no reason. The young couple are traced to the crime by the serial numbers on the banknotes Hanzaemon gave them, and they are accused of the murder. Jinnai learns of their predicament by reading the *Tōkyō Nichinichi Shimbun* and, moved to contrition, sends a telegram to the authorities confessing his guilt. He plans to take a steamship from Kobe to Yokohama and a train from Yokohama to Tokyo in order to turn himself in. Mokuami's conservative approach shows in that Jinnai's shame over his crime was inspired by hearing a Buddhist sermon on the evils of alcohol, and in that his decision to save the lives of an innocent couple reflected the Confucian samurai code, but the telegram, steamship, and train were all modern features. Moreover, Jinnai was able to travel only because an edict issued in 1871, stating that samurai were no longer required to wear swords, enabled Jinnai to sell his sword in order to pay for his passage back to Tokyo. Towards the end of this long play there is a dream sequence set in Kamakura in the days of Yoritomo in which it is revealed that Hanzaemon had accidentally killed Jinnai's father, and that Jinnai was therefore unconsciously avenging his father's death. This typical Kabuki touch of Buddhist cause and effect philosophy shows how little Western thought had penetrated this *zangirimono*.

Mokuami's achievement was to treat the new age effectively while remaining within the traditional Kabuki idiom. No doubt he was happier when allowed to write about Edo, rather than Tokyo, and the majority of his plays written in the Meiji period were still set in the past, whether they described the Soga brothers or the warfare between the Taira and the Minamoto clans. His most popular plays described the seedier aspects of contemporary life in the manner which had earned him his reputation before the Restoration. *Kagatobi* (1886), a great success, was almost indistinguishable from a pre-Meiji work, though occasional references to modern fashions lent an amusingly anachronistic flavor.

Mokuami also turned to the West for direct inspiration. In 1879 he wrote *Ningen Banji Kane no Yo no Naka* (The World of Human Beings Where Money is Everything), a comedy based on *Money*, the 1840 play by Bulwer Lytton. He transferred the scene of the action from London to Yokohama and changed the names of the characters. [Alfred] Evelyn became Efu Rinnosuke, his fiancée Georgina became Oshina, and his devoted cousin Clara became

Okura. Mokuami's adaptation of the Western play ran for two months. The foreigners of Yokohama were so touched by his interest in Western drama that they presented a curtain to the theater.

In the same year Mokuami toyed with the notion of making a Kabuki adaptation of *Hamlet*. He visited Yokohama to see some foreigners perform the play, but eventually decided against adapting *Hamlet*, though he incorporated certain passages in later plays. This decision was probably dictated by the disastrous failure of his most conspicuous attempt to achieve the Meiji ideal of the blend of East and West, *Hyōryū Kidan Seiyō Kabuki* (The Wanderers' Strange Story: A Foreign Kabuki; 1879). The work contained a play within a play, a musical drama sung and acted out by an English troupe from Hong Kong. Although summaries of the foreign play were distributed, the spectators were baffled by the Western acting techniques, and to the Japanese, unfamiliar with the sound of the Western language, English sounded like the noise a chicken makes when its neck is wrung. It proved that Japanese audiences were not yet ready for Western musicals.

It was hard for Mokuami to accept the new ways, but as a genuine professional he wrote whatever the actors or the public demanded of him. There was very little he could not do. Tsubouchi Shōyō once described him as "the grand wholesaler of the Edo theater, the Western Roman Empire of Tokugawa popular literature," and characterized Mokuami's works as a "metropolis." This is exactly the impression we still receive today when we come in contact with this extraordinary dramatist's work.

TŌKAI SANSHI

1852–1922

At the time of the Meiji Restoration the intelligentsia scorned fiction as far beneath their dignity and considered it a mere entertainment for illiterate women and children. It was not until translations of European novels began to appear after 1877 that a new conception of the value of fiction and the functions of the novelist reached Japan. The translation of the novel *Ernest Maltravers* by Bulwer Lytton, called *Karyū Shunwa* (Spring Tale of Blossoms and Willows) in Japanese, was published in 1879 and not only impressed the Japanese with its serious political overtones, something inconceivable in a work of *gesaku* fiction, but also with the exalted position of the author, a Member of Parliament who had been elevated to the peerage for his services to the nation. Translations of novels by Disraeli created an even profounder impression. If the prime minister of what was then the greatest nation in the world was not ashamed to write fiction, surely it could not be despised as a mere plaything. Sakurada Momoe (1859–83), the first Japanese to consider himself to be a political novelist, declared that the novel was the best means available to patriotic citizens who wished to enlighten the people and reform society. When Itagaki Taisuke visited Victor Hugo in 1882, he was advised that political novels could serve a valuable purpose in a country like Japan. Before leaving France, he heeded this advice and purchased a large number of such novels.

The prestige of Western literature, especially of political novels, impressed the samurai intellectuals, and the growth of political activity in Japan helped to lay the groundwork for a new litera- ture. In 1874 the first political party was formed, and although there was no national parliament where its members could air their views, the organization was capable of swaying public opinion. The Satsuma Rebellion hindered the growth of liberal thought, but the Freedom and People's Rights movement con- tinued to grow in strength. In 1880 a hundred men, representing 87,000 people from all over the country, drew up a petition calling for the immediate convening of a national assembly.

In the same year the first Japanese political novel *Jōkai Haran* (Storms in the Seas of Passion) by Toda Kindō (1850–90), ap- peared. It is ironic that the pioneering work of a serious literary movement should have been so trivial. The political philosophy in this work is essentially that of freedom and people's rights, but this is almost impenetrably concealed under the frivolity of the typical *gesaku* style.

O-ken (Miss Rights), a geisha of the Sakigake (Leaders) House, is in love with a customer named Wakoku Minji (Japan's Popular Government). He is attracted to O-ken, but has long had relations with another geisha, Hikutsu-ya Yakko (Slave of the House of Servility), and finds it hard to break with her. A rich merchant named Kokubu Masabumi (Correct Documents of the National Capital) makes advances to O-ken, but she spurns him. In the end,

after many difficulties, Minji and O-ken are married, and Masabumi, graciously yielding to the inevitable, arranges the wedding
reception at a place called Kokkai (National Assembly). This
foolish work is of some importance, not only because it was a
first attempt in Japan at a political novel, but because Toda Kindō
was the first member of the upper-class intelligentsia to have
written fiction.

The incipient Meiji political novel acquired distinction with the
publication in 1883 of the first part of *Keikoku Bidan* (Inspiring
Instances of Statesmanship) by Yano Ryūkei (1850–1931). Ryūkei's father, a progressive scholar who was well read in both
Chinese and Western learning, had encouraged his son's interest
in foreign countries by reading to him *Robinson Crusoe* in translation. In 1868 Ryūkei, then aged 18, served as a guard at the
imperial palace in Kyoto during the turbulent days of the Restoration. Two years later the family moved to Tokyo, and the
following year Ryūkei entered Keiō University where he performed brilliantly. In 1880 Ryūkei and some friends from Keiō
drew up a mock constitution for Japan, based on the English
constitution, calling for elections at the close of 1882 and for the
convening of a parliament the year after. These plans were
supported by Ōkuma Shigenobu, the Minister of Finance, and in
October of 1881 the emperor answered Ōkuma's petition by
declaring that a parliament would be convened in 1890.

Ryūkei, a loyal follower of Ōkuma, worked so assiduously to
organize the Kaishintō (Progressive Party) that his health suffered
and he was confined to a sickbed in the spring of 1882. This
enforced leisure had a beneficial effect: Ryūkei used it to plan a
novel that would promote public acceptance of the tenets of the
Kaishintō. He knew that the rigid censorship of the press and
books would not permit any publication to appear which
described the current political situation. He decided therefore to
draw his materials for *Inspiring Instances of Statesmanship* from
ancient Greek history.

Inspiring Instances of Statesmanship is a cross between a history and a novel. The events described are scrupulously documented with references to textbooks of Greek history, but Ryūkei handled his materials freely and on the whole succeeded in making ancient Greece seem of immediate relevance to Japanese readers, some of whom only fifteen years earlier had demanded expulsion of all foreigners in a frenzy of xenophobia. Young intellectuals identified themselves with the noble Thebans, and some were even inspired to write novels themselves; Tsubouchi Shōyō was so impressed that he decided to pursue a literary career after reading Ryūkei's novel.

The next important political novel was *Kajin no Kigū* (Fortuitous Meetings with Beautiful Women) by Shiba Shirō, who was usually known as Tōkai Sanshi, the Wanderer of the Eastern Seas. He was the son of an Aizu clan retainer and had taken part in the battle of Toba Fushimi in 1866. In 1868 he was captured and imprisoned after the capitulation of the Aizu clan to the imperial forces. In later years he described his experiences in these terms: "At the age of fourteen I lost my country, lost my house, lost my mother, lost brothers and sisters, and our family income was confiscated by the government. My father and elder brothers were incarcerated in different parts of the country, and I, as the vassal of an enemy of the Court, was deprived of all protection and guidance. I had no money, no friend to help me, and I wasted my time in meaningless activity here and there in dire poverty, never becoming formally educated. I consequently never studied poetry or prose with others, nor did anyone teach me. I might be described as a self-made man."

Despite these adverse circumstances, Tōkai Sanshi strove constantly to improve himself. He studied English and later became the houseboy of an Englishman in Yokohama. In 1877 he enlisted in the army and served as a temporary officer during the Satsuma Rebellion. Some letters he wrote describing the fighting were printed in a Tokyo newspaper, and he was made the official historian for the brigade. The acquaintances he made at this time helped him to go to America in 1879, where he entered the University of Pennsylvania. In 1884 he received the degree of Bachelor of Finance from the university.

While in America Tōkai Sanshi became absorbed with the political crises abroad—the efforts of the Irish under Parnell to obtain home rule from England, the Egyptian uprising of 1882 led by Arabi Pasha (1839–1911), and the struggles of the Carlists in Spain. He worried that Japan might also be in danger in this age of rampant imperialism. He wrote his brother in Japan that he planned to compose a political novel and even mentioned the title, *Fortuitous Meetings with Beautiful Women.*

This is how the novel begins:

"Tōkai Sanshi one day climbed the steps of Independence Hall in Philadelphia. He saw above him the cracked Liberty Bell, below him the Declaration of Independence. He reminisced about the noble character of the American people in those days when, raising the battle standard of justice, they had rid themselves of the tyrannical rule of the English king and eventually succeeded in becoming independent and free. Now looking up, now looking

Independence Hall in Philadelphia

down, he was overcome with emotion. He gazed out the window with a deep sigh. Just at this moment two young ladies came up the spiral stairs."

Tōkai Sanshi is attracted by the two beautiful women, but being preoccupied by his musings on the American Revolution, he does not address them. He leaves without learning their identity, but by the kind of happy accident in which this novel abounds, he sees them again on the Delaware River when their boat goes by, one lady plying the oars, the other playing a concertina. He encounters them again at Valley Forge, but hesitates to violate etiquette by introducing himself. At this point one lady approaches. Here is Tōkai Sanshi's description: "She was 23 or 24 with green eyes, white teeth, and long blonde hair. (Western people consider that a woman with green eyes and lustrous blonde hair is beautiful.) . . . In attitude and appearance she brought to mind pear blossoms wet with dew or crimson leaves floating in an azure pond."

This lovely creature addresses Tōkai Sanshi: "Your hair is black and your eyes flash. I wonder if you might not be a Spanish gentleman." "No," he replies, "I am Tōkai Sanshi, and I have come to this land with a pack on my back." The lady asks in surprise, "Then have you come from the capital of Fusō, the Land of the Rising Sun?"

The lady identifies herself as Kōren (Colleen) and declares that she and her friend have taken refuge at Valley Forge. She comments with self-satisfaction, "Truly I have built a magpie bridge over the Delaware to permit a wandering star to cross."

Tōkai Sanshi approaches the other lady. She looks like the new moon seen through a veil of clouds, but on closer inspection she seems more like a dazzlingly white crane poised on fairy steps. She is perhaps twenty and, though not heavily made-up, her cool loveliness might be mistaken for snow. Her eyebrows are blue as the paintings of distant mountains; her phoenix sidelocks are greener than the clouds; the autumn waves in her eyes, brimming with feeling, are piercingly clear, yet conceal a majesty in their depths; her crimson cheeks are wreathed in smiles; and her lips part to reveal sparkling teeth. Tōkai Sanshi's heart leaps, his chest heaves, and he can scarcely bow. Soon he is smitten with this lady, whose name is Yūran (Yolande), and he listens to her tale of woes. Her father, a Spanish gentleman, has devoted his life to the Carlist cause and is the enemy of the corrupt Queen Isabella II. He was denounced and sentenced to death, but escaped to America. The other lady, Tōkai Sanshi learns, is from Ireland, and she describes her country's long suffering at the hands of the English.

In the next chapter it is the turn of Yūran's Chinese servant, Ting Fan-ching, to relate how he fled to America in order to escape Manchu oppression only to discover that the Americans loathed him like a boa constrictor and despised him even worse than a black man. Yūran interposes at this point to deliver an encomium of Japan. She assures Tōkai Sanshi, "Your country has reformed its old government and, borrowing from Europe its good features, has discarded the bad. . . . Its strength towers in the East like the morning sun rising in the eastern sky. Its sainted sovereign will bestow a constitution, and the people have sworn to requite his sacred wisdom." She predicts that Japan will free Asia.

Next Tōkai Sanshi is persuaded to tell his story, based largely on the author's own experiences. By the time he has finished, the sun has disappeared behind the western hills and a new moon shines in the trees. They all sing a Chinese translation of the *Marseillaise* together. Carried away by the music, Yūran takes Tōkai Sanshi's hand and begins to dance with him. Later, as he is eating dinner, he hears a voice call his name and beg him not to leave. He discovers that it is a parrot who addressed him. Kōren asks, "I wonder who taught the parrot to say those words?" Yūran looks down and says nothing.

But no matter how much love tempts Tōkai Sanshi, his duty to study revolutionary movements constantly keeps him traveling.

Only after many adventures in America and Europe does he return home, convinced that Japan has the mission of preserving Korea from Chinese aggression. At the end he sets forth on his travels again, this time to Egypt, in search of Yūran.

As the above extracts indicate, *Fortuitous Meetings with Beautiful Women* is written in a puerile mixture of old-fashioned Japanese and Chinese phraseology combined with an artless presentation of different examples of Western political events. As we read the novel, it is hard to suppress a smile as again and again beautiful women confess their love to Tōkei Sanshi only for him to direct his gaze away from them toward his destiny as a wanderer in search of revolutions. Yet there is something extremely moving also about a Japanese author of the middle Meiji period who described with great concern the suffering of fellow men, from Korea to Ireland. Tōkai Sanshi is proud of his country, but there is no suggestion that he finds the Irish, Spanish, Chinese, or Hungarians he encounters alien. Nor does he suppose that foreigners are incapable of understanding the griefs of a Japanese. Despite its childishness, this novel possesses a vision of Japan more elevated than that of most later writers. Its idealism is appealing, especially in the faith the author shows that Japan will one day be a strong, compassionate, and democratic country.

The political novels came to an end in 1890 when the Diet was convened. Some novelists, like Tōkai Sanshi, became Diet members, and they inevitably felt disillusioned when they observed at first-hand the factionalism and clashes of interest that occurred. Tōkai Sanshi, whose early photographs showed him in an Egyptian fez and tunic, in his later photographs appears in formal court dress. He had an undistinguished though successful career in the Diet. His only lasting monument was *Fortuitous Meetings with Beautiful Women*, a work that not only expressed the high ideals of the author but helped pave the way for the triumphs of later Japanese fiction.

HIGUCHI ICHIYŌ

1872–1896

Among the literatures of the world, Japanese literature is the only one where women played a major role in the creation of early masterpieces. Women writers can usually be omitted from discussions of most varieties of European literature before the nineteenth century; and their role in Chinese literature was minor as well. But it would be impossible to discuss Japanese literature without mentioning works by women such as *The Tale of Genji*, *The Pillow Book*, *The Gossamer Years*, the *waka* of Ono no Komachi and Princess Shikishi, and many other writings of the Heian and early Kamakura periods. Even in the *Manyōshū* women poets were prominent, and it was their poetry which set the tone for later *waka* not only by women but also by men.

Of course this literary phenomenon was closely related to the social position and education of these women writers. They were well-educated court ladies who were hardly inferior in social status to the men. Unlike the men of the court, however, they were not expected to learn Chinese, and if in fact they learned it, they generally were at pains to avoid revealing this unladylike accomplishment. The men wrote poetry in Chinese, more by way of demonstration of scholarly ability than as an outlet for their emotions, but the women continued to write in Japanese, most often in the *waka* form. By the ninth century the invention and widespread adoption of *kana* eliminated the clumsy *Manyōgana*, and it became far easier to compose Japanese poetry now. The *kana* came naturally to be associated with women, while the men, as before, used the Chinese medium in writing, and it was therefore left to the Heian court ladies to express the creative genius of Japan during a period when the civilization was especially brilliant.

The changes in society brought about during the Kamakura period by the feudal regime tended to cause women to play a less and less significant role in literary composition. During the centuries after *Izayoi Nikki*, written in 1280 by the nun Abutsu, and *Towazugatari* (Confessions of Lady Nijō), written after 1306, hardly a single work by a woman left its imprint on Japanese literature. It is true that the court ladies continued to compose *waka* and novels written in imitation of the Heian traditions until the fifteenth century, and that in the Tokugawa period a few women enjoyed reputations for their *waka*, *haiku*, and even *kanshi*, but their works, with extremely few exceptions, are of minor significance only. The handful of works written by women during the Muromachi and Tokugawa periods did little to change the overall situation in Japanese literature, though the group of extraordinary women writers in the Heian and early Kamakura periods had shaped all of Japanese literature. Whether the writer of a *waka* was a man or a woman, the style and manner of composition was tinged by the femininity of the Heian period. The melancholy of a rainy evening, the preciousness of beauty that soon would fade away, the unspoken overtones of a casual remark, and other characteristics of the feminine sensibility of the Heian period became the heritage of the entire Japanese people.

The revival of feminine literature did not take place until the Meiji period. The long-standing prejudices against education for women that had persisted during the feudal period began to give way to more enlightened views, partly in response to Western influence. Girls were among the students sent abroad by the government, and they were admitted to the educational institutions founded at home. Their role in literature at first was modest. The nun Ōtagaki Rengetsu (1791–1875), the best-known woman writer of the early Meiji period, is remembered today only for a few *waka* and for some paintings whose charm reflected little of the new epoch.

Women poets became prominent in the later Meiji period, but there was only one woman prose writer of first importance, Higuchi Ichiyō, who, indeed, ranks among the major authors of the period. Ichiyō's fiction, at once sensitive and realistic, has earned her so high a place that voluminous studies have appeared which painstakingly examine her short life in detail in the hopes of discovering how a woman with so little formal education and so little contact with other writers managed to achieve such great distinction. Ichiyō's diaries are also of importance, not only for what they reveal about her life, but because these autobiographical records, selectively and poetically set down, restored the diary, one of the oldest genres of Japanese literature, to its former distinction.

Ichiyō was the daughter of an ambitious farmer who had gone up to Edo from the country shortly before the Meiji Restoration and purchased status as a samurai. Ichiyō was proud of this "samurai ancestry," dubious though it was, and liked to think of herself as an impoverished gentlewoman, a victim of the changes brought about by the Meiji Restoration. Ichiyō's schooling came to an end when she was eleven. This was not for lack of ability—she stood at the head of her class—nor even because of poverty, but because her parents, typically for the time, were sure that too much book learning was undesirable for a girl and might make it impossible for her to marry. Ichiyō was permitted, however, to study the *waka*, a suitable accomplishment for a young lady, and in 1886 she entered the Hagi-no-ya, a school run by Nakajima Utako (1841–1903), a leading *waka* poet. Not only did Ichiyō learn to write *waka* in the faded style of the late Keien school, but she received instruction in such classics as the *Kokinshū*, *The Tale of Genji*, and *Essays in Idleness*. These studies conspicuously affected her prose style, especially that of her diaries, which were written throughout in a style reminiscent of the Heian period, even though the incidents described are often strikingly modern.

At the Hagi-no-ya Ichiyō became friends with Tanabe Kaho (1868–1943), the daughter of a distinguished statesman. Kaho had shown a precocious interest in *gesaku* fiction, and had delved into Saikaku's works and Washington Irving's *Sketchbooks*. The rediscovery of Saikaku in the late 1880s directly influenced the style and manner of Kaho's *Yabu no Uguisu* (Nightingale in the Grove), the first noteworthy story by a Meiji period woman. In this work Kaho condemns the indiscriminate adoption of Western values.

Nightingale in the Grove, revised and with an introduction by Tsubouchi Shōyō, was published in 1888. No doubt the eminence of Kaho's father helped her to find a publisher for her story. It was generally praised, perhaps because it appeared just as the reaction had set in against the adulation of the West symbolized by the Rokumeikan, a hall where Japanese and foreigners met socially and danced together. The heroine's superficial infatuation with the West leads to her downfall. She betrays her fiancé, a man of impeccable virtue, by taking up with her English tutor, a scoundrel interested only in her money. The construction of the story, hardly impressive by our standards, was condescendingly praised for its complexity—considering that the author was a woman! The style combined dialogue in the colloquial with descriptive passages written in a *gesaku* style of classical Japanese.

The success of *Nightingale in the Grove*, especially the reports that Kaho had received thirty-three yen in royalties for her manuscript, aroused Ichiyō's envy and ambition, and she set out to do the same. Her first literary compositions, written in 1890, were prompted by the financial crisis in her household precipitated by her father's death in the previous year. Throughout her career Ichiyō wrote primarily to support herself and her family, and even her brief romances seem to have been inspired by the same purpose.

In April of 1891 Ichiyō paid a call on the journalist and hack novelist Nakarai Tōsui (1860–1926). She had apparently not read his novels, but sought him out anyway, probably because he was the only author accessible to her. A friend at the Hagi-no-ya school knew Tōsui's sister and, if we can believe what Tōsui later wrote, Ichiyō was at the time doing the laundry for the Nakarai family. Ichiyō described this visit in her diary:

> "His greetings when we first met were friendly, but I was still a novice at such encounters that I felt my ears grow hot and my lips become dry, and I couldn't remember what I had intended to say. Totally incapable of speech, all I could do was to bow profusely. It embarrasses me when I think what an idiot I would have looked like to any outsider."

Ichiyō was favorably impressed by Tōsui's appearance, and listened attentively as he spoke disparagingly of contemporary fiction. He wondered what he should write, considering the childish tastes of Japanese readers who did not appreciate serialized fiction unless the author strung together the usual tales of plotters and bandits or else related the doings of wicked women and prostitutes. He admitted that he took no pride in the novels he had recently published, and was unable to look critics in the face when they attacked his works. But what was he to do? He wrote not in the hopes of fame but in order to feed and clothe his parents, brothers, and sisters. Some day he hoped to publish a novel after his own taste, and if that happened he probably would not be so tolerant of criticism.

Tōsui's remarks accurately conveyed the predicament of novelists at the time. Unless their works appealed even to badly educated readers, they could not hope to earn a living, no matter how highly they were praised by the discriminating few. Tōsui was primarily a reporter, and the writing of the novels serialized in the *Asahi Shimbun* was part of his job, not a conscious artistic effort. Ichiyō went to see him because she dreamt of earning enough money from her writing to be able to give up sewing and washing clothes. She seems to have fallen in love with Tōsui at first sight, but her love never blinded her to his inadequacies as a writer nor to the possibility of using him to advance her career.

Tōsui agreed to read a manuscript by Ichiyō, and she left with him the first installment of a story. When she visited him a few days later his only comments were to note that the installment was too long to be published in a single issue of a newspaper, and that the Heian flavor of her style was somewhat excessive. This was typical of the assistance he gave her. However, Tōsui promised to introduce her to various scholars. Ichiyō was far from discouraged by his apparent lack of enthusiasm for her work. She was more impressed by Tōsui than the first time. Tōsui, though friendly, seems not to have contemplated any romantic involvement.

Ichiyō visited Tōsui frequently during the following year, ostensibly for consultations about her writings, but seemingly more attracted by the man than by his teachings. Tōsui cautioned her that her visits were likely to cause gossip, but she paid no attention to his warnings. In her diary she deplored her own forwardness, wondering how she, who had always been so timid, had become so brazen.

The first stories written under Tōsui's guidance were published in the magazine *Musashino*, which he founded. They do not reveal great talent, and the marks of Tōsui's influence, such as the excessive emphasis on surprising twists of plot, indicate that her choice of a mentor was unfortunate. Nevertheless, Tōsui confidently predicted that Ichiyō would become famous one day. Realizing that someone better placed than himself was needed at this stage in her career, Tōsui promised to arrange a meeting with the celebrated novelist Ozaki Kōyō (1867–1903). But before the meeting could take place, Ichiyō was warned by a friend from the Hagino-ya school that she must break with Tōsui if she valued her reputation. Ichiyō had previously heard rumors about Tōsui's profligacy, but they seem not to have disturbed her. Now, however, gossip had it that she was his mistress. Horrified, she swore she was innocent of any improper behavior. Two days later she learned from Nakajima Utako that Tōsui had referred to Ichiyō publicly as his "wife." She declared her innocence and her intention of breaking with Tōsui.

Ichiyō lacked the courage to tell Tōsui the bad news all at once. On her visit the next day she merely declined his offer of an introduction to Kōyō, and only a week later did she tell him of the rumors and of her decision not to meet him for the time being. Tōsui agreed to the separation, but hoped they might meet again when the rumors had died down.

Ichiyō's diary, in which the above events are recorded, is so movingly written that it is easy to see why some critics have praised it as her finest work. Wada Yoshie, a specialist who devoted much time to Ichiyō, once suggested that the diary should be read not as plain truth but as autobiographical fiction. He believed moreover that Ichiyō, having realized it was useless to hope that Tōsui would get her stories published in the important literary magazines, used the gossip about their relationship as a pretext to break with him. Viewed in this light, Tōsui appears to have been the victim of Ichiyō's fierce ambition.

This harsh interpretation of her motives is open to dispute, but there is no doubt but that her diary at times deviated from the truth, especially when she described her relations with men. She was not only reticent, as we might expect of a proper young lady of the Meiji period, but she had a writer's natural tendency to make her diary into a work of literature. When her stories were at last recognized and acclaimed she neglected the diary, probably because she no longer needed this outlet of thoughts and emotions too complex for the conventional fiction she wrote at the outset of her career.

Ichiyō was discovered by the literary world only after *Takekurabe* (Growing Up) appeared serially in *Bungakkai*, beginning with the January issue in 1895. Her story was highly praised by all the leading figures of the day, including Mori Ōgai and Kōda Rohan, but even such men could not resist the temptation to add condescending remarks, such as, "If you concealed the name of the author, nobody would ever guess the story was written by a woman."

During the last months of her life, when she was too ill to write, a steady stream of visitors came to her sickroom to pay their respects. In July of 1896 she took to her sickbed, and four months later she died, at the height of her fame, not only considered the first woman writer of distinction for many centuries but, thanks to *Growing Up*, the finest writer of her day.

MASAOKA SHIKI

1867–1902

Almost all the literary critics of the early Meiji period agreed
that the *waka* and *haiku* had outlived their usefulness. The sorry
state of both poetic forms bore out this judgment. By this time,
not a single first-rate *kajin* or *haijin* was active. Such eminent *kajin*
as Tachibana Akemi and Ōkuma Kotomichi had died on the eve
of the Meiji Restoration. The *haiku* was in a much worse state;
the last important *haijin*, Kobayashi Issa, had died nearly fifty
years before. The *waka* and *haiku* composed during the first years
of the Meiji period were generally insipid, hardly more than
variations on familiar themes which had been stated innumerable
times by earlier poets. A few poets, both of *waka* and *haiku*, attempted to describe the changes ushered in by the new regime, but
such works tend to be comic rather than evocative. This *waka*
addressed to students of foreign learning was typical:

yoko ni hau   Even though you may learn
kani nasu moji wa   The crab-writing
manabu to mo   That crawls sidewards,
naoki mikuni no   Never forget
michi na wasure so   The True Way of Japan.

There were *tanka*[1] on newspapers, foreign umbrellas, ice-sellers, thermometers, gas lamps, hospitals, the Yokosuka shipyards, and policemen. These topics were certainly a far cry from those of the *Kokinshū* poets or from the imitations of the *Kokinshū* by *kajin* of the Keien school, but apart from their obviously "poetic" features, such as the *makurakotoba* or archaic grammatical forms, these *tanka* could scarcely be described as poems.

It does not take extensive reading in such poetry to reach the conclusion that it was not possible to adapt the *tanka* and *haiku* to the new age. In 1882 three young men who had absorbed the new learning published *Shintaishi-shō* (Collection of Poems in the New Style). The preface by Inoue Tetsujirō (1855–1944) conveyed the scorn of these advocates of new poetry for the old forms: "The old *waka* are not worthy of consideration. Why not write poems in the new form?" Inoue and his colleagues insisted that the *tanka* could not cope with the modern world. Tsubouchi Shōyō three years later voiced the opinion that the men of former times were able to compress their thoughts into a mere thirty-one syllables because they themselves were basically simple men, but that modern people are so much more complex that they cannot be content with such a limited number of words.

A study of Western poetry and theories of poetry convinced various Japanese that the *tanka* was no more than a plaything for dilettantes. For example, the preface to *Jūni no Ishizuka* (The Twelve Stone Tablets; 1885) by Yuasa Hangetsu (1858–1943) urged poets to abandon the *tanka* and create new poetic forms, rather than attempt to improve the *tanka*. One critic, writing in 1888, deplored the limitations of the *tanka* and declared that the *kajin*, in the attempt to convey *mono no aware*, had sacrificed philosophical and aesthetic depth. He proposed that formal restrictions on poetic expression be dropped, that the classical language in poetry be replaced by contemporary speech, that the subject matter be vastly expanded beyond what was hitherto considered the domain of poetry, and that the Japanese write narrative and allegorical poetry and even poetic dramas.

Many similar views appeared in the literary journals of the 1880s and 1890s. The intimate connections between the *tanka* and the old aristocracy were decried by men who were involved in the new political currents. They called for democratic poetry which would describe life in Meiji Japan in modern language, and which would be filled with an optimistic, masculine spirit in place of the melancholy, effeminate tone of the old poetry.

The *haijin* of the years immediately after the Restoration were even less concerned with modern society than the *kajin*. The first event to disturb their serene indifference to change was the decree at the end of 1872 proclaiming the adoption of the solar calendar as of the following January 1. Of all the varieties of Japanese poetry, the *haiku* was the most closely associated with the seasons, and the adoption of the new calendar was extremely upsetting to the poets. New Year did not occur at the beginning of spring now but in the coldest part of the winter, and the Tanabata Festival no longer brought the first cool breeze of autumn since, according to the new calendar, it was to be celebrated in the middle of July.

Apart from such matters, the *haijin* seemed unaware of how stale and even meaningless much of their art had become. They rejoiced in the undiminished number of pupils and in the respect which *haiku* commanded. In 1873, for example, the Ministry of Instruction charged four *haiku* masters with the task of making the *haiku* conform to the new policies of the state. Bashō was established as a legitimate object of worship in 1879, and elaborate commentaries on his *haiku* demonstrated that he had preached the Confucian virtues. In 1885 the government recognized the Furuike Kyōkai (Church of the Old Pond) as a religious body affiliated with the Bashō sect of Shinto. The name of this church was, of course, a reference to Bashō's best-known *haiku*, on the frog jumping into the old pond.

Despite this official protection, the *haiku* was not immune to sharp attacks from advocates of the *shintaishi* (poems in the new style). But there were also some who were convinced that the *shintaishi* would not flourish in Japan because it was basically alien to Japanese tastes. A contemporary critic wrote, "We Japanese seem to love nature more than artifice. The Europeans and Americans desire perfection, but we Japanese seem to prefer things that have not yet attained this state. The Europeans and Americans love excitement, but we Japanese prefer quiet." The cries of those who sought to destroy the *tanka* and *haiku* as unwelcome vestiges of the past and those who sought to preserve uniquely Japanese forms of poetic utterance cancel one another out. It was left to Masaoka Shiki to restore the importance of both *tanka* and *haiku* by giving to them a new significance for modern Japanese.

Shiki was trained mainly in the Confucian classics during his formative years in Matsuyama. This training seems to have occasioned his rational outlook on the world, and it might have been expected that Shiki, like others who had received a samurai education, would have expressed himself most successfully in the *kanshi*, but he preferred *haiku* and *tanka*. He became accomplished in both of these chosen forms, though one may suspect that he was temperamentally suited to neither.

Shiki's intelligence, fostered by his Confucian education, was one of two dominant factors in his life; the other was his illness. In 1888, Shiki, then a student in Tokyo, after being caught in a heavy rain, twice coughed up blood. This was the first sign of the illness that would take his life at the young age of thirty-five. In 1890, he again coughed up blood, and on this occasion wrote a series of poems about the *shiki*, a bird described in Chinese legends as having coughed up blood.

The unmistakable signs of an illness that was usually fatal did not seem to have depressed Shiki greatly. His journal *Bokuju Itteki* (A Drop of Ink) is full of passages revealing a love of life and a passionate concern for poetry. The following account, written in 1891, is typical:

"Towards the end of the year I rented a house in Komagome where I lived by myself. The place was extremely quiet and ideal for studying, but somehow I could not bring myself to face the subjects of my examinations. The only thing I read were *haiku* and novels. Two days before the examinations I finally began my preparations. As I sat there quietly before my desk, transformed from a chaotic mess into neatness itself, it gave me a pleasant feeling, so pleasant, so buoyant in fact, that *haiku* kept bubbling up inside me. I opened a notebook, but before I could read a page a poem had already formed in my mind. I wondered what I could write it on, since I had carefully removed every blank notebook or sheet of paper from the desk. So I wrote the poem on the lampshade. Then another one came to me. And another. It was so much fun that I gave up all pretense of studying for the exams, and before long I had covered the lampshade with *haiku*."

These *haiku* apparently have not been preserved, but judging from others written by Shiki about the same period, they were probably not of great literary value. Indeed, we cannot but be struck by the discrepancy between the keen judgments Shiki passed on other men's poetry and his own curiously unpoetic spirit. He was perceptive and intelligent, but he lacked the lyric intuition associated with the *tanka* and *haiku*. In place of beauty of tone, suggestion, and other traditional values, he attempted to make clarity and strength the marks of excellence, both in his own poetry and in that of others. This insistence on objectivity and precision of language may have been the only way for him to write poetry, given his severe, unemotional character.

Shiki's first major statement of his views on *haiku* was presented in a series of articles published in 1892 under the title *Dassai Shooku Haiwa* (Haiku Chats from the Otter's Studio). The most interesting section of the work contains his predictions for the future of *haiku*. He opened this section with a reference to mathematics, typical for a man of the enlightened new age: "Present-day scholars who have studied mathematics say that the number of *waka*, *haiku*, and similar forms of Japanese poetry is unquestionably limited, as one can calculate easily from the number of permutations possible with a mere twenty or thirty syllables. In other words, the *waka* (by which is generally meant the *tanka*) and the *haiku* must sooner or later reach their limits. We have already arrived at the point where it is quite impossible to compose a wholly original poem." The innumerable *tanka* and *haiku* composed since the distant past all seem different at first glance, but on careful examination it becomes apparent how many are alike. Pupils plagiarize works of their teachers, and men of later generations plagiarize creations of their predecessors. Shiki was sure that both *tanka* and *haiku* would meet their end during the Meiji period.

This statement was far more sweeping than any previous attack on traditional Japanese poetry. Shiki did not merely point out the inadequacies of traditional poetry when it came to expressing the life of the new age, but insisted that it could no longer fulfill any literary function. The *tanka* could not respond to the changed times, he felt, because of its rigorous insistence on purity of diction, and the *haiku*, though it did not absolutely reject new words, certainly did not welcome them. Shiki was extremely pessimistic about the future of the *tanka* and *haiku*, but his concern in fact saved them from the demise he predicted.

In 1893 the two-hundredth anniversary of the death of Bashō was celebrated. Shiki seems to have been irritated by the excessive adulation offered Bashō that year, and he was inspired to write in *Bashō Zatsudan* (Miscellaneous Chats on Bashō) what was probably the harshest criticism ever directed at the "Saint of *Haiku*." He opened his discussion of Bashō's "bad poems" with a deliberately provocative statement: "I should like to state at the outset my judgment that the majority of Bashō's poems are bad or even doggerel, and not more than a tenth can be called first-rate. Even barely passable verses are as rare as morning stars." The only *haiku* by Bashō he praised unreservedly was the well-known one on the frog jumping into the pond. But he admitted that Bashō had written some *haiku* that possessed masculinity and grandeur, the two qualities he thought were most lacking in Japanese literature. Shiki's essay on Bashō exudes the brashness of youth, and no one could accept all of his judgments, but even his mistakes effectively awakened people from their complacent Bashō-worship. Henceforth Bashō's defenders would have to prove his excellence.

Shiki's essays, written between 1894 and 1896, reveal his steadily increasing admiration for Buson. His long essay *Haijin Buson* asserts, "The *haiku* of Buson are equal to Bashō's and in some respects superior. He has failed to win commensurate fame mainly because his poems are not for the common people, and because the *haiku* poets after Buson were ignorant and lacking in discrimination." Shiki was particularly impressed by Buson's pictorial qualities. He learned from the painter in the European style, Nakamura Fusetsu (1866–1943), the principle of *shasei* (copying nature), and under his guidance he not only learned to distinguish Japanese and Western paintings, but he reached the conclusion that the *haiku* and painting were in essence identical arts.

Shiki's activities as a critic earned him his reputation as the founder of the modern *haiku*. His own *haiku* are far superior to any written for the previous fifty years, but few are of absolutely first quality. The famous ones include:

kaki kueba	As I bite into a persimmon
kane ga naru nari	The temple bell tolls at
Hōryūji	Hōryūji.

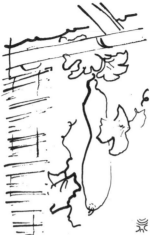

A sponge-gourd in flower

ikutabi no	Again and again
yuki no fukasa wo	I asked the others about
tazunekeri	The depth of the snow.
hechima saite	The sponge-gourd has
tan no tsumarishi	flowered!
hotoke kana	Look at this Buddha
	Choked with phlegm.

The third haiku was written the day before his death, on September 19, 1902.

Only during the last four years of his life did Shiki devote his attention to the composition of *tanka* and *tanka* criticism. The prolonged illness of his last years did not prevent him from engaging actively in meetings of the Negishi Poetry Society or from rediscovering such forgotten *tanka* poets as Tachibana Akemi. In his last years Shiki could not leave his bed. His world was limited to his room and the corner of the garden visible from his pillow. Despite his insistence on *shasei*, all he normally saw of nature was the flowers brought by visitors. A series of ten *tanka* on wisteria contains some of his best *tanka*, beginning with:

kame ni sasu	The wisteria cluster
fuji no hanabusa	Thrust into the vase
mijikakereba	Is so short
tatami no ue ni	It does not reach
todokazarikeri	As far as the *tatami*.

Shiki was the leading force in the revival of both *haiku* and *tanka*. Both forms seemed doomed to disappear at the beginning of the Meiji period, but forty years later they were flourishing, thanks to a man whose short life was spent mainly in a sickroom. Shiki's career was a paradox: he was an unpoetic poet, an anti-traditionalist who saved tradition, a man of feeble health who restored the health of Japanese poetry after a long period of sickness.

NOTE

1. The terms *waka* and *tanka* denote exactly the same poetic form, a poem in thirty-one syllables arranged in five lines. *Tanka*, meaning "short poem," came to be the usual term during the Meiji period.

GLOSSARY

bummei kaika—"Civilization and Enlightenment," a slogan used by those who advocated the adoption of Western technology and thought at the beginning of the Meiji period.

bunjin—"A man of letters," the dilettante ideal of many Japanese poets and painters, especially of the eighteenth century, who rejected professionalism.

chōka—A long poem in Japanese. The form, seen to best advantage in the eighth-century anthology *Manyōshū*, was revived in the eighteenth century after long neglect.

gesaku—A general term for the prose fiction composed from about 1770 to 1870; it means literally "playful composition," a term originally intended to indicate that the author disclaimed responsibility for a work.

haijin—A poet who writes *haikai* verse.

haikai no renga—The comic style of *renga*, practiced by even serious *renga* poets of the Muromachi and Sengoku periods by way of diversion.

haiku—A term invented late in the nineteenth century to designate a poem which is complete in seventeen syllables and is not thought of as the opening verse of a comic linked-verse sequence.

hōin—A high-ranking Buddhist title.

hokku—The first verse of a linked-verse sequence.

jidaimono—Plays, generally based on historical facts, which depict the grandiose actions of people of the past.

jiyū minken—"Freedom and People's Rights"—the ideal of liberal-minded people in the early Meiji period.

jōruri—The puppet theater, called Bunraku since the early nineteenth century; also used for the plays performed at this theater which are sung and recited by a *tayū* to musical accompaniment.

Kaishintō—The Progressive Party, a political party founded in the early Meiji period which advocated the establishment of a constitutional government along the lines of that of Great Britain.

kajin—A poet who composes *waka* (or *tanka*).

kambun—Prose composed by Japanese in classical Chinese.

kampaku—Chancellor.

kanshi—Poetry composed by Japanese in classical Chinese.

kanzen chōaku—"Promotion of virtue and chastisement of vice"—the ostensible object of many nineteenth-century works of fiction and drama.

kasen—"The immortals of poetry"—a term that came to denote a sequence of *haikai no renga* or *renku* in thirty-six links, so called because there were thirty-six "immortals of poetry."

kawaraban—Broadsheets giving a fanciful or literary description of some recent event, usually illustrated.

kinsei—"Recent age"—used more or less synonymously for the Tokugawa period, 1600 to 1867.

kogiha—"Original meaning school"—a branch of Tokugawa period Confucianism which insisted on the importance of going back to the original texts, rather than read them in conjunction with later commentaries.

kokkeibon—"Funny books"—the designation of a variety of humorous *gesaku* works of the nineteenth century.

Kokinshū—"Collection of Poems Ancient and Modern"—probably the most influential of all the imperially sponsored anthologies; compiled in A.D. 905.

koku—A measurement of rice, about five bushels; the stipends of samurai were usually stated in terms of the number of *koku* received from their superiors.

kokugaku—"National learning"—the study of the Japanese classics, especially the *Manyōshū* and *Kojiki*; flourished in the eighteenth century.

kyōka—A comic variety of *waka*.

kyōshi—A comic variety of *kanshi*.

maeku—The "previous verse" in a linked-verse sequence.

Manyōgana—The system of writing originally used to transcribe the Japanese sounds of the poems in the *Manyōshū*. It consisted essentially of using a Chinese character for its sound alone, without consideration for its meaning. Some of the *Manyōgana*, in a highly stylized and abbreviated form, were adopted for the two sets of *kana* in use today.

Manyōshū—The great anthology of Japanese poetry, compiled in the eighth century. The pronunciations and even the meanings of many poems were lost when *Manyōgana* ceased to be used, and the value of these poems was not appreciated until the scholarship of the seventeenth century and later made them intelligible again.

michiyuki—The journey section of a play or work of fiction, often relating, with references to places passed on the way, the feelings of suicidal lovers on their way to death.

mono no aware—The "pity of things"—a term used especially by Motoori Norinaga to describe the sensitivity of people to emotional experiences.

nengō—Reign name used in pre-Meiji Japan to designate periods of an emperor's reign.

ninjōbon—Works of *gesaku* fiction which emphasized romantic attachments.

renga—The art of linked verse.

renku—Linked verse composed in Chinese, rather than Japanese; also, linked verse associated with Bashō and his followers.

ryō—A silver or gold coin; its value varied widely between the sixteenth and nineteenth centuries, depending on the content of precious metal.

sengoku—The name commonly given to the period of warfare of the sixteenth century; the dates of this period are variously given: almost all who use the term agree that the period began in 1467, with the outbreak of the Ōnin War, but the conclusion is given by different authorities as 1568, 1573, 1590, and 1603. I have used the term in this book to correspond, more or less, to the sixteenth century.

seppuku—Ritual disembowelment.

sewamono—Domestic tragedies which described events in the contemporary world, especially those relating to the townsmen and lower ranks of samurai.

sharebon—A form of *gesaku* fiction largely devoted to describing the pleasure quarters.

Shin Kokinshū—"New Collection of Poems Ancient and Modern"—perhaps the most beautiful of the imperially sponsored anthologies; second only to the *Kokinshū* in its influence. Compiled in 1205.

shintaishi—Poetry in the new style; that is, poetry not in traditional Japanese forms but composed under Western influence.

shosagoto—A dance play, with little or no dialogue, performed as part of a Kabuki program.

shōsetsu—A word commonly translated as "novel," though it includes not only short stories and novellas but sometimes works of non-fiction.

sōrōbun—The epistolary style; used not only in letters but in the Nō plays. It is characterized by the use of the verb *sōrō* for the copula.

tanka—The name by which the *waka* came to be known generally during the Meiji period.

tayū—The narrator of a puppet play; the same word had other uses, including the designation of the highest rank of courtesan.

tengu—A long-nosed goblin known for its mischievous and sometimes malicious pranks; believed to live in the mountains.

togaki—Stage directions, but by extension came to mean also passages in works of fiction in which the manner of speech or actions accompanying speech are characterized.

tsukeku—The verse appended to a *maeku* by another poet.

uta—A general name for poetry, but used especially for the *waka*, the classical verse form in thirty-one syllables.

wakiku—The second verse of a linked-verse sequence.

yūgen—A quality in works of literature much sought by *waka* poets and Nō dramatists especially; its meaning changed in the course of time, but generally it meant an elusive, mysterious beauty.

yūkaku—The pleasure quarters; in the Tokugawa period the brothels, restaurants, and theaters associated with the *yūkaku* were often described in works of literature.

ADDITIONAL READING

Arntzen, Sonja. *Ikkyū Sōjun: a Zen Monk and his Poetry.* Bellingham, Wash., Western Washington State College, 1973.

Beichman-Yamamoto, Janine. "Masaoka Shiki's *A Drop of Ink,*" in *Monumenta Nipponica,* XXX, No. 3, 1975.

Brower, Robert H. "Masaoka Shiki and Tanka Reform," in Donald H. Shively, (ed.) *Tradition and Modernization in Japanese Culture.* Princeton, Princeton University Press, 1971.

Brower, Robert H. and Earl Miner. *Japanese Court Poetry.* Stanford, Calif., Stanford University Press, 1961.

Hall, John Whitney and Toyoda Takeshi. *Japan in the Muromachi Age.* Berkeley, University of California Press, 1977.

Hisamatsu, Sen'ichi. *Biographical Dictionary of Japanese Literature.* Tokyo and New York, Kodansha International Ltd., 1976.

Isaacson, Harold J. *Peonies Kana: Haiku by the Upasaka Shiki.* New York, Theatre Arts Books, 1972.

Keene, Donald. *Landscapes and Portraits.* Tokyo and New York, Kodansha International, 1971.

Keene, Donald. *World Within Walls.* New York, Holt, Rinehart and Winston, 1976.

Miner, Earl. *An Introduction to Japanese Court Poetry.* Stanford, Calif., Stanford University Press, 1968.

Miner, Earl. *Japanese Poetic Diaries.* Berkeley and Los Angeles, University of California Press, 1969.

Sansom, George. *A History of Japan.* 3 vols. Stanford, Stanford University Press, 1958–63.

Ueda Makoto. *Literary and Art Theories in Japan.* Cleveland, The Press of Western Reserve University, 1967.

Varley, H. Paul. *Japanese Culture.* Revised Edition. New York, Praeger, 1977.

ORIGINAL TEXT OF POEMS
AND QUOTATIONS

p. 20 　　有漏地より　無漏地へ帰る　ひと休み，
　　　雨降らばふれ，風吹かばふけ.

p. 21 　　住庵十日意忙々
　　　脚下紅糸線甚長
　　　他日君來如問我
　　　魚行酒肆又婬坊　　　　　　　　　　（『狂雲集』）

p. 22 　　　　題婬坊
　　　美人雲雨愛河深
　　　樓子老禪樓上吟
　　　我有抱持睫吻興
　　　意無火聚捨身心　　　　　　　　　　（『狂雲集』）

p. 23 (1) 　　自戒
　　　罪過彌天純藏主
　　　世許宗門賓中主
　　　說禪逼人詩格工
　　　無量劫來惡道主　　　　　　　　　　（『狂雲集』）

　　(2) 木凋葉落更回春
　　　長落生花舊約新
　　　森也深恩若忘却
　　　無量億劫畜生身

　　(3) いづれの人か骸骨にあらざるべし. それを五色の皮につゝみ
　　　てもてあつかふほどこそ, 男女の色もあれ. いきたえ, 身の
　　　皮破れぬればその色もなし, 上下のすがたもわかず. たゞ今
　　　かしつきもてあそぶ皮の下に, このがいこつをつゝみて, う
　　　ちたつとおもひて, 此の念をよくよくこうしんすべし.

　　　　　　　　　　　　　　　　　　　　　　（『骸骨』）

p. 32 　　打払ふ　床のあたりに　おく太刀の

さやかにいづこ　曇る塵なき

p. 33 (1) ねがはくは　なき名は立たじ
　　　　われ死なば　八十あまりを　神も知らじよ

　　　(2) いかにせむ　物書きすさぶ
　　　　手はおきて　箸とる事と　尻のぐふ事

p. 34 稚児か女か　ねてのあかつき
　　　　まへうしろ　さぐる手に月の　有明に
　　　　人のなさけや　あなにあるらん　女ふみ
　　　　かしこかしこに　かきすてて

p. 37 童形なれば，何としたるも幽玄なり．声も立つころなり．二
　　　　つの便りあれば，悪き事は隠れ，よき事はいよいよ花めけり
　　　　（『花伝書』）

p. 38 大和猿樂の兒童，去頃より大樹之を寵愛し席を同じくし器を
　　　　傳ふ．かくの如き散樂は乞食の所行なり．しかるに近仕に賞
　　　　翫する條，世以つて傾寄の由．財産を出し賜はつて物を此の
　　　　兒に興ふるの人は，大樹の所存に叶ふ．仍つて大名ら競つて
　　　　之に賞賜し，費巨萬に及ぶ．　（『後愚昧記』）

p. 39 声もすでに直り，体も定まる時分なり……よそ目にも，すは
　　　　上手出で来たりとて，人も目に立つるなり．……人も思ひあ
　　　　げ，主も上手と思ひしむるなり．これ，返々，主のため仇な
　　　　り．これも，まことの花にはあらず，年の盛りと，みる人の
　　　　一旦の心の珍しき花なり……　（『花伝書』）

p. 42 因果妄執，思ひの涙，砧にかければ，涙はかへつて，火焔と
　　　　なつて，むねの煙の，炎にむせべば，さけべど声が，いでば
　　　　こそ，砧の声なく，松風も聞えず，苛責の声のみ，おそろし
　　　　や（『砧』）

p. 44 治部入道其時八十餘の大入道にて，白髪ぶきなるが出で逢ひ
　　　　て申し侍りしは，「兒の哥あそばさるゝ事は，今の時分更に
　　　　無き事なり，禪薀が若盛りの時などにてこそ，さやうの事は
　　　　承りしか．やさしき御事也．是に毎月廿五日に月次侍り．御

出で候ひてあそばし候へ．今月の題は，是これにてさふら
ふ」といひて，我と書きてくれ侍り．深夜閑月・鵙・別無書
戀，三首四文字の題にて有りし也．それは八月始めつ方の事
也．さて廿五日に會に罷り出でしかば，一方の座上には，冷
泉の爲尹・爲邦，今一方の座上には，前探題，その次つぎに
近習の人達，禪薀が一族共卅餘人，歴々としてなみ居たる所
へ，遅れ出でしかば，横座へ請ぜらるゝ程に，計會にて有り
しかども，座敷へつき侍りし．探題は其時八十餘の入道にて，
墨の裳なし衣に，ひんがうたいの房の長きをして居給ひしな
り．深夜閑月は，

いたづらに更け行く空のかげなれや
獨り詠むる秋の夜の月

鵙の哥は，「山の端に一つら見ゆる初鵙の聲」と有りしやら
ん，上を忘れ侍り．戀も覺えざる也．それからひた出でにい
でもてきて，哥を讀みならひし也．その頃十四歳にて有りし
也．其後奈良の門跡へ奉公し侍りし比ほひ，むろ山の講堂供
養に上童にて供奉しなどして奉公にひまもなかりし程に，し
ばらく哥を讀まざりき．其後，親にをくれ侍りしから，又さ
し出でて哥を詠み侍りし．治部が所の會よりこなたの詠草
が卅六帖有りし也．二萬首餘有るべき也．それを皆今熊野に
て燒き侍りし也．其後，今までの詠草が一萬首にちと足らぬ
物也．（『正徹物語』）

p. 48   咲けば散る夜のまの花の夢のうちに
やがてまぎれぬ峯の白雲

幽玄躰の哥也．幽玄と云ふ物は，心に有りて詞にいはれぬも
の也．月に薄雲のおほひたるや，山の紅葉に秋の霧のかゝれ
る風情を幽玄の姿とする也．是はいづくか幽玄ぞと問ふに
も，いづくといひがたき也．それを心得ぬ人は，〔月は〕きら
きらと晴れて普き空に有るこそ面白けれといはん道理也．幽
玄といふは更にいづくが面白きとも妙なりともいはれぬ所
也．「夢のうちにやがてまぎれぬ」は，源氏の歌なり．源氏，

藤壺に逢ひて,

　　見ても又逢ふ夜稀なる夢のうちに

　　　　やがてまぎるゝ憂身ともがな

と讀みしも, 幽玄の姿にて有る也.　　　（『正徹物語』）

p. 49　寺はあれど　昔のままの　飾りなき

　　　仏となりて　山ぞあせゆく

p. 56　人は三十歳のうちに名を發つせざれば, 立身ならぬ物なり.
　　　つくづくと, 世の有様を見るに, 連歌師はやすき道と見えて
　　　職人町人も貴人の御座につらなれり.　　　（『戴恩記』）

p. 58　年々の　花ならぬ世の　恨かな

　　　ふりにしあとも　夜の春草

　　　山の端の　うす雪のこる　露みえて

p. 59　旅枕　夢ぢたのむに　秋の夜の　月にあかさん　松風の里

p. 60　(1)　二本手に入る　けふのよろこび

　　　(2)　舞ひあそぶ　千世萬世の　扇にて

　　　(3)　洛中の老若, それを聞いて, 何とも物をば言はず. この人は,
　　　　たけき武士なれば, 寿永の古へ, 木曾が京入りしたるやうに
　　　　こそあらめと思ひしに, 優にやさしうもありけるよな. さて
　　　　は安き事もあるべきにやと, 心の中, たのもしうなつて, 皆
　　　　息をぞやすめける.　（『信長記』）

p. 61　時は今　天が下しる　五月哉

p. 66　今は只　恨みもあらず　諸人の　命にかはる　我身と思へば

p. 67　もろ共に　消はつるこそ　嬉しけれ　後れ先だつ　習なる世
　　　を

p. 69　大閤大相国, 本朝を心のままに治め, 三韓を平げ, 剰へ唐土
　　　よりも懇款を入るるにより（中国からの和平の懇願を受諾し
　　　た）, 武勇功を終へ還御ならせ給ひ, 山城の国伏見の里に大
　　　宮作し給へり. 又この春は吉野の花見として御参詣の御事な

れば，只今供奉仕り候．（『謡曲三百五十番集』）

p. 70　　あまの刈る　藻に棲む虫の　われからと音をこそなかめ　世
　　　　をば恨みじ

p. 74　　いにしへも　今もかはらぬ　世の中に　心のたねを　残す言
　　　　の葉

p. 75　(1)　問．女郎花とよみて，花と，また一首のうちによむべきか．
　　　　答．よむべきなり．

　　　(2)　ただ，月の花といふことに心を付けたるがよきなり．その上
　　　　に，無常を心にかけて歌をよむべし．その他は広く求めても
　　　　いらぬことなり．

　　　(3)　からたちは　やがてそのまま　きこくかな

p. 76　(1)　「うへさまと同年」と申さる．「扨は午の年か」と仰られけ
　　　　れば，「午のとしには候へどもかはりたるむまにて侍る」と
　　　　申されければ，「なにとかはりたるとはいふぞ」と仰らるゝ．
　　　　「上さまは金覆輪のくらをき馬，私は小荷駄馬にて，つねに
　　　　せなかにをひ物たえず」

　　　(2)　奥山に　紅葉踏みわけ　鳴く螢

p. 82　　伏見の城をせめけるに，城には若狭少将，鳥井の何がしあり
　　　　けるに，鳥井は家康公の臣なれば，此時うち死したまひけり
　　　　となん，少将は城をさり給ふてけり，時の人武勇のすすまざ
　　　　りける故をいひつたへ侍れども，こころある人の申るは，
　　　　此時治部少（石田三成）に同心したまへば家康公との信の道
　　　　たがひぬ，城にゐたまへば，宗廟の臣のみちたがひ侍り，し
　　　　かあるゆへに，世をすて山に入たまふことは宗廟の臣の道も
　　　　たがはず，朋友の信の道もかけ侍らぬは，そのためし，もろ
　　　　こしにはありぬべければ，聖賢の道をまなびたまふ故にやと
　　　　いへり．

p. 83　　常に住所はかはらふけるものふたつ，函丈二間をば殊にしつ
　　　　らひて，みぎりのかべに杜少陵が詩，古人の和歌，あはれな
　　　　るは色紙にかきてをしつ．みづからのつたなきことの葉もお
　　　　りにふれたる情すぐさぬはかたはらにかきつく．人みるべき

ならねばことにかたくななるもつみゆるしつべし．やがて愛を半日とす．客はそのしづかなることをうれば，我はそのしづかなることをうしなふににたれど，おもふどちのかたらひはいかでむなしからん．（『山家記』）

p. 85 (1) かどさして　八重むぐらせり　我が宿は都のひがし　わしの山本

(2) 松風は　吹きしづまりて　高き枝に　又鳴きかはす　春のうぐひす

(3) 世々の人の　月に眺めし　かたみぞと　思へば思へば　物ぞかなしき

p. 86 つゆの身の　きえてもきえぬ　おき所　くさ葉のほかに　又もありけり

p. 88 中にも迷惑せしは，ある山川の岩波たぎりて，かち渡り思ひもよらざるに，ただほそきひとつばし有けるを，をさなき子は右の手にてかかへ，丸（貞徳の号，延陀丸）があねの六つばかりになりしを，左の手にてひき，よこざまにそろそろと渡られしを，こなたのきしより，それも子供を前うしろにいだき，見やりたれば，橋の半にて父の顔の色，下の水よりもあをくみえしと，後に母の物語有しを，いま思ひ出すに，父母の心のうち思ひやられてかなしくこそ侍れ（『戴恩記』）

p. 90 (1) 花に猶　みちわけそへん　行衛哉　　　　　　　植通

(2) はるはかすみに　ひかれぬる袖　　　　　　　　貞徳

(3) たかとはふ（とぼう）　すそののききす（雉子）　鳴捨て

　　　　　　　　　　　　　　　　　　　　　　　　　幽斎

p. 100 この道や行く人なしに秋の暮

p. 101 切られたるゆめはまことか蚤のあと　　　　　　其角
去来曰く『其角は誠に作者に侍る．わづかに，のみの喰ひつきたる事，たれかかくは謂ひつくさん』．先師曰く『しか

り. かれは定家（ていか）の 卿也（きよう）. さしてもなき事を，ことごとしく
いひつらね侍る，ときこへし評に似たり』（『去来抄』）

p. 102　蚊をやくや褒姒（ほうじ）が閨（ねや）の私語（ささめごと）

p. 103　(1)　塩鯛の歯茎も寒し魚（うお）の店（たな）

　　　　(2)　声かれて猿の歯白し峰の月

p. 112　浄るりは憂ひが肝要也とて，多くあはれ也なん どいふ文句
を書き，又は語るにも，泣くが如くかたる事，我が作の い
きかたにはなき事也. 某は憂ひはみな義理を専ら とす. 芸
の六義が義理につまりてあはれなれば，節（ふし）も文句 も きつと
したる程いよいよあはれなるもの也. その 故に，あはれを
あはれ也といふ時は，含蓄の意なふしてけつく其の 情うす
し.

p 114　(1)　身は人くづと，いはばいへ. わらばわらへ. 一すぢに思
ひそめたる恋なれば，たとへ此の身をつらぬ かれ，ほねは
ことなれはひとなれ. こんな此の世にとどまりて，かげに
つきそひ身にうつり，二世も三世も我がつまと手に手 を と
りて，れんげのり.

　　　　(2)　おろかにござる吉三様. 我が心からなすわざを少し もくや
む事ならず. あふてしぬれば今ははや心にかかる事はなし.
おまへは命めでたふし. 御出家なされなきあとを，よくよ
くとふて下さんせ.

p. 121　　　　霜曉
曉枕覺時霜牛晞
滿窓晴日已熹微
臥看紙背寒蠅集
雙脚挼挲落復飛

p. 122　(1)　溪村無雨二旬餘
石瀨沙灘水涸初
滿巷蟬聲槐影午
山童沿戶賣香魚

(2) 南軒有待不燃燈
四壁蟲聲夜氣澄
指點前峰留客坐
愛看大月抱松升

p. 123 茶山ノ詩ノ躰ハ，六如ニ本ヅケルモノナリ．六如ガ詩ハ，
景多クシテ情少ナク，濃密ニ過ギタリ．始メ喜ブベシト雖
モ，後ニ厭ヒ易シ．茶山ハ情景相半シ，濃淡中ヲ得タリ．
故ニ久シクシテ厭ハザルコトヲ覚ユ．

p. 124 山陽の京師に出でんとするや，廉塾の壁に
山凡水俗　先生鼈，弟子愚
と題して去りぬ．その廉塾に在るや，常に茶山を目して禿
頭と呼びけるが，ある日外より帰り，同塾生に向ひ『禿頭
は内に居るか』といへるに，茶山羽織袴を着けて恭しく襖
を開き，『菅太仲ここに在り』といひつつ出でるに，山陽
その意外なるに驚きて，覚えず地に伏して拝したりといふ．

p. 126 秋の夜のほがらほがらと天の原てる月影にかりなきわたる

p. 129 古人は師なり，吾にあらず．吾は天保の民なり，古人にあら
ず．みだりに古人を執すれば，吾身何八，何兵衛なること
を忘る．意のうはべのみ大臣の如くなりて，よむ歌さぞ尊
きことにてもあるべけれども，そは賢人の冠袍を着たるな
る．全く真似にて，歌舞伎を見るが如し．

p. 130 日のひかりいたらぬ山の洞のうちに火ともし入りてかね掘
出す

p. 131 (1) 赤裸の男子むれゐて 鉱 のまろがり砕く鎚うち揮て

(2) たのしみは戎夷よろこぶ世の中に皇国忘れぬ人を見るとき

(3) 真荒男が朝廷思ひの忠実心眼を血に染めて焼刃見澄す

p. 132 妓院雪
庭の雪たはれまろがす少女ども其手は誰にぬくめさすらむ

218

与女見雪
おんなとゆきをみる

妹とわれ寝がほならべて鴛鴦の浮きゐる池の雪を見る哉
おしどり

p. 133 (1) いつはりのたくみをいふな誠だにさぐればうたはやすから
いも
むもの

(2) たのしみはまれに魚煮て児等皆がうましうましといひて食
うお こ
ふ時

p. 136 雅言にて實情を委く云うつす事は得がたし．和歌にて俳諧
のごとく日用の事はいひ取りがたしと見ゆるなり．云得た
れば至て妙所なり．中華にて俗語小説ものにては，委細に
情がうつり易し．……源語勢語淫書なれども雅なるやうに
書し故，今の上留理本八文字屋本ほどに情がうつらず．（儒
医の勝部青魚著『剪燈随筆』の一節）

p. 138 女（かほをのぞいて見て）ヲヤ ぬしやァ寝なんすかへ を
きなんし をきなんし（トかほへたばこのけぶをふきかける）
客（けぶにむせながら）エヘン エヘン ゆふべから ま
んじりともしねへから（ト又ねぶる）
女 いやだよ ねかしやァしねへよ 晩にねなんしな サア
目をあきなんし あきなんし（トはなをつまむ）

p. 142 元来予著はす草紙，大略婦人の看官をたよりとしてつづれ
もとよりわが おおかた
ば，其の拙悝なるはいふにたらず．されど姪行の女子に似
て，貞操節義の深情のみ．一婦にして数夫に交り，いやし
くも金の為に欲情を発し，横道のふるまひをなし，婦道に
欠けたるものをしるさず．巻中艶語多しといへども，男女
の志清然と濁なきをならべて．

p. 145 文政三年十月朔日夕七時なりけるが，屋代輪池翁の来まし
て，山崎美成が許に，いはゆる天狗に誘はれて年久しく，
其使者と成たりし童子の来り居て，彼境にて見聞たる事ど
もを語れる由を聞くに，子のかねて考へ記せる説等と，よ
く符合する事多かり．吾今美成がり徃て，其童子を見もと
する也．いかで同伴し給はぬかと言はるるに，余はも常に
さる者にただに相見て，糺さばやと思ふ事ども種々きき持
ただ

たれば，甚嬉しくて……．

p. 150 月の状は，近くに寄るほど段々大きに なり．寒気身を刺ごとく厳くて，近くは寄難く思ゆるを，強て二町ほどに見ゆる所まで，至りて見たるに，又思ひの外暖なる ものなり．さてまづ光りて見ゆる所は，国土の海の如くにて， 泥の交りたる様に見ゆ．俗に兎の餅つきて居る と云ふ所に，二ツ三ツ穴あきて有り．然れど余程離れて見たる故に， 正しく其体を知らず．

p. 151 (1) 月の光る所は， 国土の海の如しと云こと， 西洋人の考へたる説もありて，然る事に覚ゆれども， 兎の餅つきて居る如く見ゆる所に，穴あきて有しと云こ と 心得がたし．彼所はこの国土の岳の如く聞ゆるをや．

(2) あなたの説は，書物に見えたる事をもて宣う故に違ふなり．我は書物は知らず．近く見て申す事なり．……正しく穴二ツ三ツ有りて，其穴より月の後なる星の見えた りしなり，然れば穴ある事疑ひなし．

p. 156 天子遷都布寵華
東京兒女美如花
須知鴨水輪鷗渡
多少簪紳不顧家

p. 157 雙馬駕車載鉅公
大都片刻往來通
無由潘岳望塵拜
星電突過一瞬中

p. 158 化政極盛日　　　　　十分善持盈
才俊各馳聲　　　　　耳只聽歌聲
果然文章貴　　　　　目不見甲兵
奎光太照明　　　　　餘澤及花木
上下財用足　　　　　各墅爭春榮
交際心存誠　　　　　人非城郭是
宇內如圓月　　　　　我亦老丁令

p. 159 (1) 莫求杜牧論兵筆
　　　　且檢淵明飲酒詩
　　　　小室垂幃温舊業
　　　　殘樽斷簡是生涯

　　(2) 渾頭漆黑髮蒙肩
　　　　下馬店門垂柳邊
　　　　小女慣看先一笑
　　　　傘如蝙蝠帔如鳶

p. 160 (1) 小揚州是新島原
　　　　關訶邦土護蠻船
　　　　勸郎莫帶兩條鐵
　　　　勸郎須帶十萬錢

　　(2) 滿世夷裝士志遷
　　　　力人妓女服依然

　　(3) 宜矣看場引貴人
　　　　名優絕伎妙如神
　　　　沐猴而冠今誰笑
　　　　猿若坊中有搢紳

p. 161 車夫何早起　　　　三千石幕臣
　　　拂拭車上塵　　　　出門乘輿馬
　　　車客猶未到　　　　揭々上士身
　　　結束立凌晨　　　　今日渾忘此
　　　昔日胡爲者　　　　快載商買人

p. 170 一此小冊子僕が例の筆頭に成る一時の戯作と雖 看官の注意
に因て又開化の一端を踏むに至らん文章の卑俗き ハ 田童野
婦に解読易からんを要とすればなり 一無用 の 書を著述し
て有用を補金ふ僕輩の是とする所贅語中自然微意あり 稗
史の卑きを捨ざる具眼ハ更に開化の得意たり.

p. 182 余は一四歳にして國を喪ひ，家を失ひ母を喪し，兄妹 を 喪
し，家祿私産を官歿せられて父兄は東西に幽囚せられ身は
朝敵の臣子なるを以て敢て保護教導する も のなく資力なけ

れば助くるの友なく徒らに歳月を東西飄零の間に消し,曾
て学業に従事したることなし.故に詩文を他人に学びたる
ことなく又余に教へたりといふものあらざるべし.蓋し余
は自作人物ならんのみ.

p. 183(1) 東海散士一日費府ノ独 立 閣ニ登リ,仰テ自由ノ破鐘
ヲ観,俯テ独立ノ遺文ヲ読ミ,当時米人ノ義旗ヲ挙テ英王
ノ虐政ヲ除キ,卒ニ能ク独立自主ノ民タルノ高風ヲ追懐シ,
俯仰感ニ堪ヘズ.愀然トシテ窟ニ倚テ眺臨ス.會々二姫ア
リ.階ヲ繞テ登リ来ル.

(2) 年二十三四緑眸皓歯黄金ノ髪ヲ垂レ(西人緑眸ニシテ毛髪
ノ金光アルヲ称シテ美人トナス)……其態度風采梨花ノ露
ヲ含ミ紅蓮ノ緑池ニ浴スルガ如シ.

p. 185 今ヤ貴國舊政ヲ釐革シ歐''ノ長ヲ取テ其短ヲ舎テ……其勢方
ニ旭日ノ東天ニ昇ルガ如ク東洋ニ屹立シ,聖帝與フルニ自
由ノ政憲ヲ以テシ人民誓テ聖明ニ報ゼン''ヲ期すと.

p. 191 初見の挨拶などねんごろにし給ふ.おのれまだかかること
ならはねば耳ほてり,唇かはきていふべき言もおぼえず,
のぶべき詞もなくて,ひたぶるに礼をなすのみなりき.よ
そめいか斗をこなりけんと思ふもはづかし.

p 196 横にはふ 蟹なすもじは 学ぶとも なほき御国の 道なわ
すれそ

p. 199 此年の暮には余は駒込に一軒の家を借りて只一人で住んで
居た.極めて閑静な処で勉強には適して居る.しかも学課
の勉強は出来ないで俳句と小説との勉強になつてしまふた.
それで試験があると前二日位に準備にかかるので其時は机
の近辺にある俳書でも何でも尽く片付けてしまふ.さうし
て机の上には試験に必要なノートばかり置いてある.そこ
へ静かに坐をしめて見ると平生乱雑の上にも乱雑を重ねて
居た机辺が清潔になつて居るので何となく心持ちが善い.
心持ちが善くて浮き浮きすると思ふと何だか俳句がのこの
こと浮んで来る.ノートを開いて一枚も読まぬ中に十七字

が一句出来た．何に書かうにもそこらには句帳も半紙も出してないからランプの笠に書きつけた．又一句出来た．又一句．余り面白さに試験なんどの事は打捨ててしまふて，とうとうランプの笠を書きふさげた．　（明治三十四年六月十六日）

p.200 　数学を修めたる今時の学者は云ふ，　日本の和歌俳句の如きは一首の字音僅かに二三十に過ぎざれば，　之を錯列法（パーミュテーション）に由て算するも其数に限りあるを知るべきなり，語を換へて之をいはば和歌（重に短歌をいふ）俳句は早晩其限りに達して，　最早此上に一首の新しきものだに作り得べからざるに至るべしと．　（『獺祭書屋俳話』）

p.201 (1)　余は劈頭に一断案を下さんとす．曰く，　芭蕉の俳句は過半悪句駄句を以て埋められ，　上乗と称すべき者は其何十分の一たる少数に過ぎず．否，　僅かに可なる者を求むるも寥々晨星の如しと．　（「芭蕉雑談」）

(2)　蕪村の俳句は芭蕉に匹敵すべく，或は之に凌駕する処ありて，却て名誉を得ざりしものは主として其句の平民的ならざりしと，蕪村以後の俳人の尽く無学無識なることに因れり．　（「俳人蕪村」）

p.202 (1)　柿くへば鐘が鳴るなり法隆寺

(2)　幾たびも雪の深さを尋ねけり

(3)　糸瓜咲て痰のつまりし仏かな

(4)　瓶にさす藤の花ぶさみじかければたたみの上にとゞかざりけり

INDEX